*Volumes in The New
Church's Teaching Series*

The Anglican Vision
James E. Griffiss

Opening the Bible
Roger Ferlo

Engaging the Word
Michael Johnston

The Practice of Prayer
Margaret Guenther

Living With History
Fredrica Harris Thompsett

Early Christian Traditions
Rebecca Lyman

Opening the Prayer Book
Jeffrey Lee

Mysteries of Faith
Mark McIntosh

Ethics After Easter
Stephen Holmgren

Christian Social Witness
Harold T. Lewis

Horizons of Mission
Titus Presler

A Theology of Worship
Louis Weil

A Theology of Worship

The New
Church's Teaching Series,
Volume 12

A Theology
of Worship

Louis Weil

COWLEY PUBLICATIONS
Cambridge, Massachusetts

The title *The Church's Teaching Series* is used by permission of the Domestic and Foreign Missionary Society. Use of the series title does not constitute the Society's endorsement of the content of the work.

Published in the United States of America by Cowley Publications, a division of the Society of St. John the Evangelist. No portion of this book may be reproduced, stored in or introduced into a retrieval system, or transmitted, in any form or by any means—including photocopying—without the prior written permission of Cowley Publications, except in the case of brief quotations embedded in critical articles and reviews.   .

Library of Congress Cataloging-in-Publication Data:
Weil, Louis, 1935
    A theology of worship / Louis Weil.
       p. cm.— (The new church's teaching series; v. 12)
    Includes bibliographical references.
    ISBN 1-56101-194-0 (alk. paper)
    1. Public worship—Episcopal Church. 2. Episcopal Church
    Doctrines. I. Title. II. Series.
BX5940 .W45 2001
264'.03—dc21   2001042307

Cynthia Shattuck and Vicki Black, editors.
Cover design by Vicki Black. Cover image: Octagonal central dome, Ely Cathedral, photograph by A. F. Kersting.

Scripture quotations are taken from *The New Revised Standard Version* of the Bible, © 1989, by the Division of Christian Education of the National Council of the Churches of Christ in the United States of America. Used by permission.

This book was printed by Transcontinental Printing in Canada on recycled, acid-free paper.

Second Printing

Cowley Publications
907 Massachusetts Avenue • Cambridge, Massachusetts 02139
800-225-1534 • www.cowley.org

Table of Contents

The New Church's Teaching Series

Almost fifty years ago a series for the Episcopal Church called The Church's Teaching was launched with the publication of Robert Dentan's *The Holy Scriptures* in 1949. Again in the 1970s the church commissioned another church's teaching series for the next generation of Anglicans. Originally the series was part of an effort to give the growing postwar churches a sense of Anglican identity: what Anglicans share with the larger Christian community and what makes them distinctive within it. During that seemingly more tranquil era it may have been easier to reach a consensus and to speak authoritatively. Now, at the beginning of the twenty-first century, consensus and authority are more difficult; there is considerably more diversity of belief and practice within the churches today, and more people than ever who have never been introduced to the church at all.

The books in this new teaching series for the Episcopal Church attempt to encourage and respond to the times and to the challenges that will usher out the old century and bring in the new. This new series differs from the previous two in significant ways: it has no official status, claims no special authority, speaks in a personal voice, and comes not out of committees but from scholars and pastors meeting and talking informally together. It assumes a different readership: adults who are not "cradle Anglicans," but who come from other religious traditions or from no tradition at all, and who want to know what Anglicanism has to offer.

As the series editor I want to thank E. Allen Kelley, former president of Morehouse Publishing, for initially inviting me to bring together a group of teachers and pastors who could write with learning and conviction about their faith. I am grateful both to him and to Morehouse for participating in the early development of the series.

Since those initial conversations there have been changes in the series itself, but its basic purpose has remained: to explore the themes of the Christian life through Holy Scripture, historical and contemporary theology, worship, spirituality, and social witness. It is our hope that all readers, Anglicans and otherwise, will find the books an aid in their continuing growth into Christ.

James E. Griffiss
Series Editor

Acknowledgments

A s a part of The New Church's Teaching Series, this volume on liturgical prayer shares the intention of being addressed in the first instance to newcomers to the Episcopal Church who are seeking a grounding in the fundamental aspects of the church's life. At the same time, since this volume is presenting a change of focus in the understanding of corporate worship, it may also be useful to both laity and clergy who want to achieve a better sense of the meaning of worship shared by most of those who contributed to the preparation of the 1979 *Book of Common Prayer.*

In this latter perspective, it is important to note that this volume does not stand alone. Not only is it related to other volumes in the current series, particularly Jeffrey Lee's *Opening the Prayer Book*, it also presumes the existence of the volume on worship included in the previous Church's Teaching Series published in the late 1970s that I co-authored with the late Professor Charles P. Price. Much of the content of the earlier volume had to do with historical data regarding the evolution of liturgical prayer in the life of the church in general, and specifically was concerned with material relevant to the Anglican prayer book tradition. There is no need to repeat what was said in that earlier volume; my goal here is rather to explore how in recent decades the public worship of all the major liturgical traditions has been moving tentatively toward a new mindset, a new perspective on the fundamental meaning of liturgical acts.

As much as possible, this volume attempts to explore liturgy from the angle of the person in the pew rather than from that of ordained leaders. The basic presupposition of this book is that public worship—the liturgy—is the shared action of the whole baptized community. The idea of the laity as passive observers or listeners, as in some fundamental sense secondary to the ordained in the roles they fulfill, is simply not acceptable as an understanding of Christian worship. The reason this may be asserted with such conviction is that such a secondary status linked to the laity betrays the radical inclusiveness of our baptismal incorporation into the church, the body of Christ that has assembled week after week for two millennia to offer praise and thanksgiving to God.

My understanding of liturgical worship has been shaped in recent years in a variety of contexts, not only through study but also through regular worship with the seminary community of students, staff, and colleagues at the Church Divinity School of the Pacific; in Sunday worship with the members of St. Mark's Church, Berkeley; and in various communities of Christians in many parts of the world where my work has taken me. All of these people and our shared experience of Christian liturgy have helped to shape in me a renewed and, I believe, deeper understanding of the meaning of worship in the life of faith. They have also led me to a strong conviction that Christian corporate prayer is essentially a very simple thing. It is often needlessly complicated by liturgical leaders who understand public worship more as a liturgical production than as an act of faith.

If, as this book proposes, the liturgy *is* what the original meaning of the word implied, "the work of the people," then the public worship in the majority of our parishes must be transformed. That transformation will require not merely new rites but, more importantly, a new understanding of the nature of liturgical actions as manifestations of the whole church. It is the whole baptized community that *celebrates* the sacramental rites, and the meaning of those rites pertains to the life of all the members.

This book has gone through a long stage of development, and I want to express my gratitude here to the staff of Cowley Publications for their patience during this time of gestation. I want also to express particular thanks to Vicki Black and Cynthia Shattuck for their insight in showing me where I needed to share more of my own experience and thus to flesh out more clearly the factors that have shaped the views expressed here. Their editorial advice has been of enormous help to me.

I have been blessed by the fact that I lived for many years with the quintessential "person in the pew," my mother LaRue Kemp Weil. Her comments about the liturgy always brought me back to reality by seeing the rites through the eyes of one who was neither ordained nor technically trained in liturgical studies. Her responses to poor liturgy always suggested the most basic qualities of good liturgy: Could it be heard? Could it be seen? Could it be understood? Did it engage me? Our current preoccupation with the development of new rites should not distract us from the fundamental intentions of good liturgy to nourish faith and to engage all who are gathered in a shared celebration of that faith. My mother, the person in the pew and a woman of great faith, died while this book was in preparation, and I offer it in gratitude to her memory.

Chapter One

Which Theology?

The Recovery of a Baptismal Ecclesiology

It is a Sunday morning. People are setting out from their homes for their parish church. Some live within walking distance; others travel quite some way to be at the church that they regularly attend. Many arrive before the time at which the service begins. Some have tasks to do: to prepare, perhaps, for one of the liturgical ministries as a reader or the leader of the intercessions, to set up for the adult education hour, or to brew coffee for those who gather after the liturgy is over. Some of the people are simply talking to friends in the hallway, and others are on the lookout to welcome visitors. Why have they come? What draws these people together week after week?

The most obvious response that they might offer is that they have come to worship God; they are drawn together because of their faith in God as known through Jesus Christ. Yet they are also here for each other, because what they are gathering to do is something which they do *together*, as a community of faith. Although anyone can worship God in private, Christian worship is essentially something we do together. Our private prayer flows out from its primary expression in the corporate prayer in which, week after week, we proclaim our faith in God as revealed in Jesus Christ. Our public worship expresses who we are as the body of Christ, and continues throughout our lives to be the primary visible expression of our commitment of faith.

It is in the public worship of the church that Christians have their primary experience of their identity as a faith community, as the people of God. Worship is the expression of our faith in God, the Holy One revealed in Jesus Christ, through our involvement in the liturgical action. The church's life is grounded in the mighty acts of God in the life, death, and resurrection of Jesus Christ. *That* is what we celebrate when we gather for worship. The liturgy—what it is intended to be and to do—is thus of fundamental significance for the life of faith.

My purpose in this book is to look at the experience of liturgy shared by those who gather Sunday by Sunday all over the world to celebrate together their faith in Jesus Christ. If our public worship reveals how we understand ourselves as the church, then we are obliged to scrutinize the widely diverse models of Christian liturgical prayer over the centuries. If we do, we soon become aware that among the many liturgical rites that have developed in various places over the centuries there is an essential question: Who is *doing* the liturgy? Is a particular rite expressive of the participation of *all* the members or of only a few leaders? Is it a drama in which all participate as actors, or do the ordained clergy perform for an "audience" of laity?

In other words, my concern in this book lies beneath the particularities of any one rite. The deeper question is whether or not the rite is *ecclesial*—that is, is it an act of the church? The word "ecclesial" should not be confused with the word "ecclesiastical," although they are both derived from the same Greek word *ecclesia*. Whereas "ecclesiastical" generally refers to the administrative or external aspects of church life, "ecclesial" has a much deeper significance: it refers to the essential nature of the church as the people of God, the entire community of baptized believers. When this word is used in reference to the liturgy, it is raising an important question about the understanding of a particular ritual: is it a shared action of *all* who have gathered? In asking this question we must go beyond the words that are printed on the page and ask further: how do the people and the ordained ministers understand themselves with regard to the liturgical action? The words "liturgical action" refer to more than merely the words printed in, for example, *The Book of Common Prayer.* The "liturgical action" is an inclusive term that applies not only to the text but to all the elements that contribute to the whole, most significantly to the full participation of the entire gathered community in movement, music, and word. How is this full participation enacted (or inhibited) through the particular liturgical mentality embodied in a particular liturgical celebration?

These questions help us to see how, in the history of Christian worship, we have sometimes strayed from the biblical understanding of the church as a people called together in the name of God. The people of God express that identity with a special intensity in gathering for corporate prayer, where through word and sacrament their unity in Christ is signified and strengthened. When we observe patterns of liturgical prayer in which that corporate identity is obscured, or in which one ministry is implicitly elevated above others so that the mutuality of ministry is eroded, we have rites that are inadequate for their purpose.

So our goal here is to penetrate to a deeper level of Christian worship and look beneath the rites to the purpose for which they exist. Why are the baptized people of God summoned week after week to gather with other Christians to *do* certain things together? Why are we expected, week after week, to listen again to the word of God proclaimed in scripture and in preaching; to offer prayer for the many needs of our world; and then to share together in the sacred meal that links us to Christians of every time and place, throughout history and around our world today? Why do we keep on doing this? Why do we *need* to keep on doing this? Let us begin our exploration with that question.

∽ Liturgy as a Shared Activity

In the United States, religion is often viewed as a private and individual concern, a matter of personal choice. Although our religious faith is often influenced by the church-going of our parents, by the time we are adults most Americans would say that their religious commitment and practice is a matter of individual choice. With regard to public worship, a very common attitude is that attendance at church services is optional, an opportunity to meet our own personal religious needs. We may feel that a church service can offer a focused occasion for private prayer supported by the atmosphere of a sacred space.

Our choice to attend a church service is based on our expectation of what such a service should be. Some people expect a long sermon as the primary element; others anticipate a high level of musical performance by the choir. In the American religious scene, the choice of a church often depends on entirely individualistic expectations of what a church is supposed to offer those who attend. It thus goes against the grain of our culture for the church to insist that participation in worship is not optional. Yet the consistent witness of the New Testament to the gathering of Christians "on the first day of the week" and the continuing practice of succeeding generations to gather as a people of faith "at all times and in all places" suggests that participation in the Sunday Christian assembly is more than a matter of personal choice. Instead, it is rooted in the central tenet of Christian faith in the death and resurrection of Jesus Christ.

Yet the ways in which this Sunday observance is fulfilled vary. There is, of course, an enormous diversity in styles of worship among the various Christian denominations in the United States. Some, such as the Pentecostal churches, rely greatly on spontaneity, often with heavy demands upon the charismatic gifts of the pastor. Liturgical churches, such as Roman Catholic, Episcopal, and Lutheran, are characterized by a tradition of *authorized* rites. This means that worship in those churches will follow a predictable and consistent pattern each Sunday, using liturgies authorized by the denomination. Liturgical churches usually hold the expectation that competent and recognized authorities in each denomination will from time to time revise current rites in the light of, for example, a changing cultural framework or new pastoral imperatives. But once this process of revision is complete, then the new rites are given an official status through authorization for use by all the members. Such authorized rites become a powerful outward expression of the unity of the people of a particular religious tradition. Note that such authorization is related to a set of texts and minimal ritual directions. These texts may then be embodied in various parishes and missions in a great diversity of liturgical styles, musical settings, and ritual actions.

Such a tradition of authorized ritual texts implies something about public worship that contradicts the extreme individualism of common American religious attitudes. The fact that these rites are primarily intended as corporate prayer suggests that the worship of God is an act that we undertake together, *as a people.* So when we gather for prayer, *we become the visible expression of the church as a faith community,* and not merely an assembly of individuals fulfilling acts of private devotion or seeing only to private religious needs. In corporate worship we manifest ourselves as a community united through a shared faith in Jesus as the Son of God. Through the proclamation of the word of God and the celebration of the eucharistic meal, our shared identity as the people of God is strengthened and we are sent forth from our assembly to serve the world in God's name.

As a Christian tradition for which the authorized forms for worship are a primary expression of our identity, Anglicanism has placed a great deal of emphasis on the significance of "common prayer" in the life of faith. This has not meant that different provinces of the Anglican Communion use identical editions of *The Book of Common Prayer.* Differences in history, culture, and social context have all contributed to the development of prayer books that vary one from another yet are similar in that a single volume includes all the basic rites. This explains why the prayer book tradition in Anglicanism has served as a major expression of the unity of its members around the world without requiring conformity to a single model, much less a single language.

Even when a single authorized book is the primary liturgical resource for a particular nation or province, the same liturgical rite may be celebrated in a variety of styles. Under the influence of the liturgical renewal movement Lutherans, Episcopalians, and Roman Catholics developed a breadth of styles within each that might be found in the parishes of the other traditions as well. Among opponents of liturgical change, this led to a suspicion that Roman Catholic liturgical renewal was too much influenced by Lutheran reforms, or that Episcopal prayer book reform was simply copying changes authorized by the Vatican. The truth is that all the liturgical churches have been deeply influenced ecumenically by our common study of ancient Christian liturgies and have been led to a shared commitment to certain fundamental principles.

Perhaps the most significant principle to emerge is that *the celebration of the liturgy is the shared activity of all the assembled people.* Conversely, this means that the liturgy is not the property of the clergy. It is not something that the clergy perform *for* the laity, who listen and look on but are slightly removed from the essential action, which is reserved to the clergy. The liturgy is now increasingly seen to be what the word originally meant, "the work of the people."

Today we are living in a very different cultural and social milieu from that in which the first prayer books were written. With regard to the role of the laity, the change between the sixteenth and the twenty-first centuries offers us an important example of how the liturgy has been affected. In the two prayer books of Archbishop Thomas Cranmer, those of 1549 and 1552, the participation of the laity was indeed recovered, but strictly within the limits of the social reality of the time. For example, the people were now expected to respond to the priest when he said, "The Lord be with you," whereas previously only the acolyte would have responded in the Latin Mass. In addition, the

people would now be expected to say the Lord's
Prayer along with the priest, whereas previously he
would have said it alone.

When we look at those earliest prayer books today,
the role of the laity strikes us as minimal compared to
that of the clergy, since the rites still indicate a dominant role for the ordained. Yet given the social context
of the time, together with the strong influence of
medieval piety and widespread illiteracy among the
laity, what Cranmer and other reformers were able to
accomplish marked a significant recovery of the
ancient understanding of the liturgy as the action of
the entire gathered community.

～ Baptism in the Early Church

This understanding of the liturgy, evident to us in documents of the late second and early third centuries of
the church, grew from the ancient belief that baptism
is the fundamental sacrament of identity in the body
of Christ.[1] Since the initiates of that time were not
allowed even to attend a celebration of the eucharist
prior to their baptism, the emotional impact of the rite
of baptism must have been enormous. Yet we cannot
overemphasize that the rite did not stand alone, unlike
countless baptisms of both adults and children today.
The ritual in the early church was a kind of public fulfillment of the whole meaning of incorporation into
the body of Christ. The impact of this ritual would
have been carried by the newly baptized into all their
future participation in the corporate prayer of the
community, defining the context in which the members of the church lived out their faith. Beyond the significance of the ritual itself, baptism played a larger
role: it established the shared identity of all members.

In the first centuries of Christianity, seekers were
required not just to profess their belief in Jesus as the

Christ, but to make choices about their daily lives. The profession of Christian faith they would eventually be invited to make was not a matter merely of repeating doctrinal formulas, but was something to be tested in the crucible of daily life itself. Conversion of life was seen in how one related to others, in how one earned a living, in how one could be trusted. Certain professions, such as being in the army where one might be commanded to kill, for example, or working at the "circus" (which in Roman society was a place of prostitution), were considered inappropriate occupations for Christians; thus, being baptized could involve changing professions as well.[2] Such a conversion of lifestyle took a long time because what was going on can best be understood as a process of socialization, as one's life was reordered to conform to the ideals of Christian faith. At the same time, the community to which these people sought membership could scrutinize their lives for the signs of authentic conversion.

So it was that the first test for incorporation into the church was one of lifestyle—a personal reformation enlightened by the witness of the scriptures and encouraged by members of the community. As a final stage of preparation, the primary tenets of Christian faith, such as those proclaimed in the baptismal creed (which we know today as the Apostles' Creed), were presented to the candidates during the days immediately prior to their baptism. These tenets of the faith were heard and memorized by the candidates so that as they approached baptism they would be able to state this summary of the Christian faith on their own. The baptism itself was an elaborate ritual incorporating water and oil, the imposition of hands, and the sharing of the eucharistic gifts. Yet it was more than a rite, since it came as the climax to a long period of prayer, study, and formation known as the catechumenate, through which candidates in the early church were expected to pass. It was this larger context that shaped the meaning of the ritual.

The catechumenate developed as a pastoral model for the formation of adults who were seeking membership in the church. It flourished especially during the third to fifth centuries of the Christian era, having first developed during times of persecution. To become a Christian was a serious matter, with potentially deadly consequences for both the candidate and for the community. During the times of persecution by the Roman authorities, the long period of preparation for baptism offered the community an opportunity to scrutinize the life of each candidate and to test whether they could be trusted not to betray the community and its faith. But when Christianity became a state religion during the fourth century of the Christian era, a less rigorous pattern of preparation began to emerge. In this new situation, much of the adult population was already baptized and baptism became ever more frequently associated with infants or children. Under these new circumstances the rigorous formation of earlier centuries was no longer necessary, but nothing developed to take its place in the larger context of Christian faith and practice. Thus a sense of the fundamental importance of formation in faith as an essential ministry of the church disappeared. Its loss led to a more narrow focus upon the liturgy and thus upon the ministries of those who were ordained—the bishops, priests, and deacons—as well as to an exaggerated emphasis on the sacraments and on those who celebrated them at the altar.

The catechumenate has reappeared in recent years as the contemporary church has begun to recognize that most church members have not been offered the type of Christian education that would enable them to make the deep connections between their lives and the faith they profess. For many people, attendance at the Sunday liturgy, as important as it might be for their own religious nurture and comfort, has been confined to a separate sphere, unaffected by the choices made in their daily lives. They are thus inhibited from drawing upon the power of their faith to engage the crises that we all confront in day-to-day living.

The catechumenal period of reading, study, and prayer that baptismal candidates undergo as preparation for their incorporation as members of the church through baptism remains a ministry of preparation for a Christian lifestyle. In many places the catechumenate has also been adapted to address the desire of baptized Christians who seek to renew and deepen their understanding of the baptismal vows perhaps made for them as infants. The modern catechumenate offers the parish a context in which those who are seeking baptism or a renewal of their baptismal vows may be confronted with the cost of discipleship, establishing the larger context for the *making* of a Christian that takes place ritually in the baptismal waters. This ministry of formation is essential for the integrity of the life of the church; without it the seeds of faith may remain on the surface of someone's life without ever taking root.

∾ Baptism as the Defining Sacrament

Recovering the importance of formation for Christian maturity within the wider context of pastoral care is one dimension of a much larger shift within the church's self-understanding. In recent decades we have been involved in the often painful process of moving from a model of church life dominated by clergy to one based upon the significance of the whole baptized community as the common ground of Christian identity.

The 1979 *Book of Common Prayer* mirrors that shift in one particularly significant way: this most recent prayer book revision in the American church offers a new set of liturgical imperatives based on a recovery of the significance of baptism in the lives of all Christians. Episcopalians are hearing much more about baptism than ever before. They listen to far more sermons on baptism and take part in more public celebrations of baptism at the principal service in their parish church. In many of our churches, this emphasis on baptism is linked to the recovery of the celebration of the Great Vigil of Easter, a rite that draws together the fundamental themes of Christian faith in the context of a baptismal liturgy. So the Easter Vigil serves not only as the primary annual occasion for the celebration of baptism but also as an opportunity for the entire community to renew their own baptismal covenant.

A number of years ago, the Great Vigil of Easter assumed a whole new depth of meaning for me. I took part as a visitor, expecting that the rite would be pretty much as I had experienced it in the past. Even with careful preparation and attention to music and the readings, celebrations of the Great Vigil are frequently word-bound. The powerful and basic symbols that the Vigil celebrates are all too often conveyed in minimalist terms: a modest fire lit with a pocket lighter, scripture readings proclaimed without any expression of their dramatic content, a small bowlful of water used in the baptism. But at this celebration of the Vigil, all the diverse gifts of the community were brought into its preparation and planning. The liturgy began, of course, with the lighting of the new fire from which the paschal candle would then be lit. But this was not merely a symbolic flame; this new fire was a true bonfire, and we could feel its heat and energy, and see our faces reflected in its great light penetrating the darkness. When we settled down later for the great series of scripture readings, we were offered more than words. Instead, the readings were dramatized in ways that invited us to share in their meaning through all of our senses, not just hearing. In that experience, I came to realize the purpose of the Vigil in a wholly new way. It did not stand outside of my life and the lives of those gathered with me, but articulated our journey of faith. Through it I realized that at the Vigil that year I was not where I had been the year before, nor where, by the grace of God, I would be a year hence. The rite lifted up the fundamental journey that every Christian is called to follow—a journey that assumes a public face in the initiatory process.

The model of baptism as the fundamental sacrament of identity in the church is sometimes referred to as a "baptismal ecclesiology"—that is, an understanding of the church that defines Christian community in terms of the common ground that all the baptized members share. This understanding of the church sees baptism as the defining sacrament of incorporation into its life. The shift to a baptismal ecclesiology has shaped the church in several extremely important ways.

One of the most obvious consequences of this shift is the realization that *the celebration of the liturgical rites is not the whole of the church's public life.* People have often identified the activity of the church with what is done by bishops, priests, and deacons, whereas a baptismal ecclesiology leads us to understand the church's life much more broadly. Thus we see the liturgy as one dimension of a much larger and more complex mosaic of the ways in which the church relates to the life of the world through the daily lives of its members. This does not deny that our public rites powerfully manifest the church as the assembly of the baptized, but these rites are not self-evident. For their full significance to be revealed, these rites must illuminate further levels of the church's understanding of ministry in the world through work and family life. Otherwise, the church can become merely a museum for the preservation of ancient rites.

Second, with regard to the place of the ordained in this renewed vision of the church, their particular gifts still serve an important role alongside the gifts of all members. The difference is that a high value is also placed upon the gifts and ministries of the laity that have in the past been obscured by the clerical model. A baptismal ecclesiology affirms that the gifts of the Holy Spirit are given to all members so that *ministry can be understood as shared by all of the people*, whether lay or ordained, each according to the nature of the gifts that the Spirit has given.

Finally, most Christians are so accustomed to the ways we are divided along denominational lines—as Roman Catholics, Anglicans, Lutherans—that the *essential unity of Christians* that baptism creates is often overlooked. These denominational divisions, however, are generally based on differences in church organization, especially with regard to ordained leadership, that go back to the New Testament. A baptismal ecclesiology acknowledges the diversity found in the history of Christianity, but it holds that through baptism Christians are given a unity in Christ that is more fundamental than church polity or governance. This baptismal ecclesiology thus offers a basis not only for ecumenical dialogue but also for common worship as Christians of different traditions work for recovery of the visible unity to which the one baptism compels us.

This emphasis upon baptism as the sign of incorporation into the community of faith, however, is not intended as a narrow focus upon a set of rituals. The rituals of the baptismal process are the outward expressions of an interior process that is taking place in the lives of the members of the community and of those who are being drawn to share their life. Without that interior reality the rites run the risk of being merely a ritual facade. What is being embodied in the process is incorporation into a community, a community linked by faith to all the other such communities around the world.

In this context, we should note that in recent years, a serious pastoral question has been posed regarding the traditional sequence of baptism followed by and fulfilled in communion. There can be no question historically that this pattern developed in the context of persecution, as we observed earlier. In the face of mortal danger from the authorities, the Christian community erected a kind of protective barrier so that potential traitors or even those weak in commitment would be turned away before reaching the intimate level of the church's life embodied in the sacraments. But in our contemporary culture, this situation no longer exists. The liturgies of the church are announced on public signs, and anyone who wishes may attend. There is no protective barrier today around what Christians understand to be public worship.

Our situation is clearly quite different from that of the first centuries of Christianity, and the question now posed by some theologians and pastors is whether we ought to have more flexibility regarding who may take part in the sacraments. For example, in certain contexts it may be appropriate for the

eucharist itself to be seen as the sacrament of welcome
and inclusion. In support of this, the open hospitality
of Jesus to strangers and even outsiders is invoked as
a model. Based on this perspective, some churches,
especially in large urban centers with a culturally
complex makeup, are inviting people to share the
eucharist if they are so moved in their own spiritual
journey, even if they have not been baptized. Not surprisingly, this change in practice has provoked both
support and rejection, and no real consensus has
emerged.

It is my conviction that in the majority of contexts
the traditional pattern still has much to commend it,
if we see baptism not as an isolated private event but
as a full incorporation into the life of the local
Christian community. Those proposing the new
model, however, would insist on the need for flexibility in a radically different social context in which the
sharing of the eucharist can itself be an act of inclusion that invites the stranger into a more intimate
relationship to the Christian community. That more
intimate level, then, would be the context in which
catechumenate and baptism would take place.[3]

～ Baptismal Ministry in the World

The foundation of the church's relation to the world is
its theology of the Incarnation, that God has in Jesus
Christ shared totally in our human reality. This starting point corrects some of the worst abuses in the history of Christian theology such as gnosticism, which
saw the creation itself as evil, as the source of temptation or alienation from God, with the attendant den-
igration of the human body as a burden to be thrown
off or denied. In the face of the claim of the
Incarnation, this denial of the body is strange fruit

indeed, but it has had a strong voice within both Christian theology and spirituality.

The centrality of the sacraments in the various traditions of Christian worship is a sign to the church of the goodness of the creation. The sacraments reveal that the physical world, far from being evil, is the domain of God's activity. The most common things in human life—a bath, food and drink, a human touch—can serve as the instruments of an encounter with God. They can express a deep experience of human community and be signs of God's grace in the fabric of human existence. So we may say that the starting point for a theology of Christian worship is to take the world seriously as the place where God acts. Our liturgical rites point to that activity, but they do not limit it.

This insight offers us a guiding principle for the relation of each Christian to the world: *the work of the church is not to escape the world, but to be the agent of transformation and healing whenever we encounter injustice, abuse, hatred, or indifference.* The ministry of each Christian, and of each Christian community, is found right before our eyes. This helps us to understand why, during the early centuries of Christianity, a newly baptized Christian was referred to as "another Christ." This had not so much to do with liturgical rites as with the fact that each individual Christian was called to be Christ in the place in which he or she lived. That is where ministry begins, and it is the work of every member of the church, not merely the ordained.

Christians throughout history have seen that the quality and integrity of their lives have sometimes served to attract others outside the church to join with them in the Christian fellowship. Attracting is different from proselytizing, which often involves the disparaging of another religion. When people are drawn to join in the life of a Christian community not because of argument or debate but rather because of its Christlike quality, there we see perhaps the surest sign of the presence of Christ in the lives of his followers.

When someone is first drawn to Christian faith, her life and experience are brought in a variety of ways into dialogue with the claims of the gospel. We have seen that in the early church the reordering of one's lifestyle was an integral part of baptismal preparation. Choices had to be made about how seekers would live their lives as members who share a Christian identity. For membership is not "fulfilled" in baptism: what begins there is a shared life, a living out of the implications of a shared faith. This ongoing nurture clusters around two poles, evangelization and eucharist. Although evangelization—that is, the proclamation of the Good News of God's grace revealed in Jesus Christ—is often thought of as ministry directed outside the church, as in the evangelization of the people of a foreign nation, it also takes place within the ordinary life of the church. Through evangelization, members of the church strengthen one another by witnessing to the reality and grace of God in their lives. Although evangelization has often been identified with the preaching of sermons, this is grossly inadequate because it takes place in so many ways, often most dramatically outside the liturgical celebration itself. Within the liturgy, the challenge to the preacher is to enable those diverse evangelical moments to unite and build up the common life of the faith community.

We see then that a baptismal understanding of the church does not narrowly focus on sacramental rites, but is rooted in the real world where we live. There the church proclaims in its ministry of evangelization the Christ whose life, death, and resurrection offer the key to the meaning of the whole creation. To those who respond to that proclamation, the church must offer a ministry of formation so that the full implications of faith in Christ may be claimed and lived. Thus we may speak of a baptismal theology in which all the baptized are equal and integral participants in its common life, bearing witness week after week to the God whom they acclaim as the Creator, the Incarnate Lord, and the Holy Spirit. When the Great Thanksgiving is said in each celebration of the eucharist, it is that baptismal faith being proclaimed among God's people to renew and nourish their faith. Then they are sent forth to serve the world in God's name.

〜 **The Ministries of All the Baptized**

Which theology—baptismal or clerical? I have argued for a theology of worship in which baptism into full participation in the life of the Christian community is understood as the foundation of the church's common life. This baptismal ecclesiology reveals that our familiar distinction between clergy and laity has led to an implied difference of status within the liturgical assembly. In its most extreme forms, the distinction creates a kind of schism within the baptismal community, contradicting the unity that baptism creates and that should be signified in every liturgical act. This understanding of baptism reminds us that Jesus established a community of equals. Jesus embodied this understanding of equality for his followers in the awesome gesture on the last night of his life when he took the role of a servant and knelt down to wash the feet of his disciples (John 13:3-20).

It is also important to realize that baptism is not a sign of *exclusion* but, in its full implications, of radical

inclusion. The full vision of baptism is of human soli-
darity, that all human beings are called to be members
of the one family of God. Thus, as a sign, baptism
points to something far greater and more comprehensive than the defined parameters of the church, much
less of any single denomination. This is why the
recovery of a baptismal ecclesiology is of such significance for the life of the church today as we live in an
increasingly polarized world in which religious
groups and ethnic groups and national societies define
themselves in an adversarial mode, opposing those
"others" who seem to menace their values. A baptismal ecclesiology lifts up a radical sign of the unity
of all people in their common vocation to be the people of God.

This baptismal ecclesiology presumes that baptism
creates a radical unity in the body of Christ. It
includes a wide diversity of gifts in the ministries of all
the members, and not just the clergy. The ministries of
the ordained are distinctive, but so are the gifts that
others bring to the common life of the community.
When this larger community discerns particular gifts
for pastoral leadership and care, then preparing for
ordination as a priest or deacon may be appropriate.
But the local church needs diverse gifts for the building up of its common life, and most of these gifts are
not directly related to a vocation for ordination. As
one who has taught in seminaries of the church for
almost four decades, I have a strong commitment to
the role that these institutions can play in the education and spiritual formation needed to fulfill those
necessary roles of pastoral leadership. Tragically,
however, such training often confirms candidates in
the highly clericalized understanding of the church's
life that they often bring with them from their own
parish experience. If the seminaries are to serve the

church of the future, the pattern of formation must be intentionally grounded in a baptismal ecclesiology, and must find effective ways to place the vocation to ordination within this more inclusive baptismal context.

Expectations about worship are shaped by the experience of the people who gather each week in the parish church. Even where we find different styles of worship in the same geographical area, regular attendance at our own parish shapes our sense of how worship ought to be done. One excellent example of this is the pastoral problem that arose in the Roman Catholic communion when, at the Second Vatican Council, the use of the vernacular—the everyday language of the people—was authorized for the first time for the Roman rite. After so many centuries in which the use of Latin in the liturgy had been virtually unquestioned, the change to the use of vernacular languages produced a serious disorientation among many laity and clergy. Their devotional lives in relation to the eucharist had been shaped by a single liturgical language—Latin—that had taken on a sacred aura. For Anglicans, the shift from so-called Elizabethan English to the use of a more contemporary idiom at first produced a similar disorientation among many clergy and laity alike. For people who worshiped for many years with the familiar forms of the 1928 *Book of Common Prayer*, their whole religious experience had been framed by the use of those classic texts. The new forms seemed at first to be altering the faith they grew up with, or at the very least to be too casual for use in liturgical prayer.

Such a narrow focus on the words of official, authorized liturgical texts tends to reinforce the expectation that God can only be worshiped using certain texts authorized by the clergy—and thus it follows that it is the ordained who regulate the liturgical life of the church. This model also places a strong emphasis on what we might call the performance aspect of the liturgy: the rites are *performed* by the clergy before the assembled laity, whose role is primarily one of watching and listening. This may sound like a caricature, but it is the model that dominated in liturgical practice for centuries and can still be found in parishes in which conformity to the authorized texts is the highest priority. This essentially clerical model has been a powerful influence for centuries in shaping what Christians understand liturgical worship to be: a pattern of sacred actions that clergy celebrate *for* God's people. Given its history, it is no surprise that the movement away from the clerical model has brought enormous stress and instability into all of the Christian liturgical traditions. Yet this is worth the cost if it enables us to recover the ancient and great tradition of the church in which liturgical worship has indeed been understood as the common action of all the gathered Christian community.

～ Unity in a Baptismal Church

We are living at a time when diverse understandings of the church and its worship may be seen across a broad spectrum of Christian communities and denominations. To a great degree this reflects the multicultural reality of our world as well as the fact than in all of the major liturgical traditions, the idea of one single normative model has given way to more diversity in practice. This diversity puts great pressure upon the principle so dear to Anglicans that all of our church's liturgical rites may be found in a single prayer book. Yet since life is never static, our patterns of worship always unfold within a tension between the need for continuity with the past and the need for adaptation to new realities. Prior to the recent decades of liturgical reform, Anglicanism's need for continuity had dominated for many centuries, helped by the invention of printing in the fifteenth century and the ensuing fixity of liturgical texts. In the evolution of *The Book of Common Prayer*, changes in the text were accepted slowly and were usually as minimal as possible. After all, such changes required the canonical authorization of a new liturgical book.

Decades of stability are now giving way to a period of experimentation that has disturbed some Anglicans, many of whom were accustomed to a particular style of public worship that could be found in most parishes on a Sunday morning. One hears complaints today that diversity in liturgical patterns has become too great. Sometimes this tension is felt in seemingly minor issues, such as the times when one is expected to stand or kneel in the liturgy. For those for whom kneeling has been the posture of reverence for many years, it can be a shock to find others standing at especially sacred times in the liturgy. When I was teaching at Nashotah House, for example, a visiting alumnus was disturbed to see that during the Eucharistic Prayer half of the community remained standing and half knelt down. "I don't care," he said, "whether they all stand or they all kneel, but everyone should do the same thing. Otherwise, you have disunity." I responded in surprise that I saw this flexibility rather as a sign of mutual respect for each person's piety. His comment, however, is typical of a demand for conformity that is characteristic of the clerical model, in which conformity and uniformity are thought of as signs of unity. They are also indicative of a high level of official control of the church's liturgical rites.

For many Anglicans this is a particularly serious issue: our unity is linked not only to our common use of the same prayer book, but also to the expectation that everyone will do the same thing at the same time. Certainly unity is fundamental to Christian community—fundamental, in fact, to the life of the church as a whole. But we are coming to recognize that unity does not require conformity to a single norm; it can find its richest expression in the bringing together of diversity. We must look at the question of unity within the larger context of the shift that we are exploring in this chapter, that is, the recovery of a baptismal ecclesiology and its implications for our understanding of worship in the life of the church. A baptismal ecclesiology tends to embrace diversity as a value in our worshiping communities.

As we have seen, the baptismal model places great emphasis on the faith community as the people of God. This theology sees the local assembly as the place in which each individual Christian experiences membership in the universal body of Christ, the "one holy catholic and apostolic Church." In a baptismal model the sacraments are *communal* symbols expressing the faith that the members of the community share. With this emphasis on the local community, conformity to a single authorized text is less important than the use of liturgical forms genuinely related to the community's life and faith.

An obvious example of needed adaptation of a liturgical form is found in the Prayers of the People (BCP 383-395). We may note that in the opening directions for this section of the eucharistic rite, the rubrics indicate the general subjects for which the gathered people are asked to pray. The intention is that those prayers will be created by local leaders, who will be alert both to the general needs of the church and the world and also to the particular needs of the local community. This intercessory section of the eucharistic rite is intended to be varied, taking shape in the hands of local congregations. But as I visit Episcopal churches in various parts of the nation, I find that almost relentlessly the only forms used are Forms I–VI, despite the fact that these models were intended only as examples and resources for optional use if necessary.[4] The rubric itself reads: "Any of the forms which follow *may* be used," and subsequent rubrics urge adaptation of the prayers to meet the needs of a particular community or occasion. Yet this great opportunity to relate the liturgy to the particular concerns of the congregation is usually lost or only minimally explored, as one or another of the six forms is slavishly used as if strictly required by the rite. Here is an example of needless conformity when the prayer book itself invites diversity. Uniformity is thus imposed by default since it is presumed to be the liturgical norm.

Perhaps the last thing in the world that would occur to a church full of people on a Sunday morning is that their gathering is "a theological act." They gather because they are members of a community of faith, a parish family. The vitality of their common life is expressed in their worship, their fellowship, their commitment to formation for Christian maturity, and their care for the needs of the society of which they are a part. To speak of the unity of faith that these people share, however, is not meant to suggest that they all think alike, because a healthy Christian community is a diverse community and we do not leave our diversity at the door when we gather for worship.

Unity in faith has sometimes been understood in American religious life as a somewhat narrow unity

based upon doctrinal formulations of the faith, a particular interpretation of scripture, or a shared moral
code. This narrow understanding of unity often produces division through its inability to welcome diversity as a value in the life of faith. The unity of
Christians in Christ transcends differences in understanding of the faith. It is always dangerous to iden-
tify God's truth with one group's point of view, since
each one of us receives the faith within our own life
experience and in terms of our own temperament,
culture, and upbringing. When the word of God is
proclaimed, we do not all hear the same thing; when
we share the eucharistic gifts, there is no litmus test
on doctrinal agreement. It is by the action of the Holy
Spirit that the word proclaimed is God's word to me
and the presence of Christ in the eucharistic gifts is
God's gift to me. Yet these gifts come to each of us not
merely as individuals but as members of the body of
Christ, the community of faith. What we receive in
our particularity at the same time unites us as a people in the grace of God.

During the early centuries of persecution, the goal
was for all Christians in a given area, usually in a city
or town, to meet together for a single eucharist on
Sunday under the pastoral oversight of their bishop.
This palpable experience of the corporate unity of the
whole local church was symbolically expressed in the
one loaf of bread and the one chalice of the eucharistic celebration. But with the liberation of the church,
and the end to persecution, the Christian community
grew rapidly. It soon became impossible for all to be
present at that one local assembly. This new situation
immediately posed a question: How was the unity of
these Christians to be embodied if they could not worship together each Sunday? One solution for a time
was to see their unity reflected in the ministry of their

bishop: whenever he presided, his presbyters would take some of the consecrated bread of that eucharist to other gatherings where, through necessity, each presbyter came to preside. We see in this the origin of the parish system, but even more importantly we see the church adjusting to new ways of embodying the unity of which baptism and eucharist were the signs.

This background, I believe, offers us insight into the multidenominational church in which we live. Inevitably, we gather in different assemblies. Even apart from denominational differences, the practical reality is that many different places of assembly are necessary simply because of the size of the Christian community. The ecumenical movement has helped us to see that in spite of our different traditions and our differing denominational characteristics, baptism continues to be the sign of our essential unity in Christ; eucharistic celebrations that are fundamental in the lives of most Christian communities all over the world each Sunday continue to be the realization and fulfillment of that unity. Our divisions are the great anomaly. Worship offers the promise of unity to which Christ summons us.

The grace of which word and sacrament are the instruments always remains beyond the capacity of any one rite to fully express. That grace cannot be adequately explained by even our most profound doctrinal formulations. Through our worship we must offer the best we can as our response to God's mysterious presence in our lives. This is our purpose in the liturgy, and from this perspective our public worship of God may be claimed as the source and summit of the Christian life.

Such a vision of the liturgy carries us far beyond the rote repetition of some ancient rituals that we either repeat or ignore as a matter of personal choice.

The liturgy asks us to be more than parrots reciting prayer forms in endless routine. The words and actions of the liturgy are grounded in the source of our created nature: they communicate meaning just as we use words and actions in our ordinary humanity to communicate meaning. Those words and actions express our fundamental conviction that God the Creator is the source of all that exists, including our fallible selves, and that we who bear the dignity of God's image are invited *as a people* into a life of praise and thanksgiving, a life in union with God. This is the vision to which a baptismal ecclesiology points and that the life of faith is called to embody.

Chapter Two

Who Celebrates?

Liturgy as the Work of the People

You arrive at your Episcopal parish on Sunday morning and are handed a service bulletin that lists the roles to which various people are assigned in the liturgical celebration that day. As you sit in your place and open the bulletin you notice who is scheduled to be the crucifer, the torchbearers, and the acolytes. The lay people who will read the scripture lessons and those who will serve at the altar and help administer the chalice are also listed. From experience you know that the ordained leaders who serve your parish will also be in the liturgy: at least one priest, in some parishes a deacon or two, perhaps a bishop if it is a day for the bishop's visitation. What impression does this list of participants in the service give you?

The message that this list of liturgical roles suggests to you will be deeply influenced by your own understanding of liturgy, and by the way that liturgical rites are celebrated in your parish. If your parish has embraced the baptismal ecclesiology described in the previous chapter, then you may well see the roles listed in the bulletin as representing the varied ways several of the members—lay and ordained—have chosen to exercise their baptismal gifts of ministry.

You might then see your role in the liturgy as equally vital: as a baptized member of the body of Christ, your participation in worship is the way you live out your identity as a Christian, "another Christ."

If, on the other hand, you and your parish have been deeply shaped by the clerical model of the church that has prevailed during most of the church's history, then you might see that list as more definitive. Although the clergy are assisted by a few trained members of the congregation for the "lesser tasks" of liturgy, you would see the role of the laity largely as one of listening, responding, and observing the clergy "doing" the liturgy. In other words, you would think only of the clergy as the "ministers" in the service.

Most of us fall somewhere in the middle of this spectrum of theologies, for the church is still in the process of incorporating the theology of baptism recovered from the early church into its daily life of worship. We see this shift even in the words we use to describe leadership roles in the liturgy. At the principal Sunday liturgy, for example, the rector or vicar is usually listed as the "celebrant." If it is not the rector who fills that role, then it is assigned to another ordained priest—perhaps an associate or a visiting priest—but it is always a priest who proclaims the words of the Great Thanksgiving, the eucharistic prayer by which the gifts of bread and wine are consecrated for communion. In some instances, moreover, other priests may be listed as "concelebrants," which means they will stand near the celebrant during the proclamation of the eucharistic prayer, and may even join the celebrant with words or gestures. Concelebration does not accord well with a baptismal ecclesiology since it overemphasizes the role of the ordained. Limiting the term "celebrant" and "concelebrant" to bishops and priests sends the message that only the priests are celebrating the eucharist, and fails to recognize that *all* the people gathered are celebrants. If the eucharist is truly the shared action of the whole people of God, then, in reality, all the members of the assembly are celebrants and concelebrants, not merely the priest.

In recent years an ancient term has reappeared to designate the role we have usually called "the celebrant." That term is "presider," and it refers to the ordained priest who exercises liturgical oversight of a particular eucharistic celebration. To at least some degree, the reclaiming of this term in our liturgical vocabulary is the result of the renewed emphasis on the significance of baptism shared by laity and clergy alike. When the word first began to appear in church publications several decades ago, it drew criticism from some church-goers because it seemed to echo the vocabulary of the secular world—the term "presider" seemed more appropriate at a board meeting than in an act of Christian worship.

Is this question of terminology mere hair-splitting? If so, it nevertheless points to an important issue, and one of great importance to the whole gathered community for understanding the liturgy. Who *celebrates* the eucharist? And related to this question is another: If all baptized members are the celebrants, then what is the role of the ordained in the liturgy? If we say that the priest's role is to preside at the eucharist, what is the difference between celebrating and presiding? The terms "celebrant" and "presider" imply a radical contrast in how the liturgy is seen and, consequently, how the congregation as a whole as well as the ordained understand their respective roles.

⮌ Celebrant or Presider?

The term "celebrant" developed in a context in which the ordained priest was seen as the only *essential* person for a celebration of the eucharist to take place. So extreme was this view in the later Middle Ages that a priest could say mass with only a server or even alone. From this perspective the laity were extraneous to the essential action—the offering of the eucharistic sacrifice—even though they were expected to attend. So thoroughly were the non-ordained excluded from the eucharistic action that communion of the laity became a rare event, held canonically to the minimum of once each year. Their access to the eucharist was restricted to gazing upon the Blessed Sacrament when it was elevated by the priest at the altar during the reciting of the Words of Institution. In such a context, it is quite evident how the word "celebrant" came to be narrowly identified with the priest at the altar.

This clerical model of liturgical leadership remains with us today, and not only are clergy resistant to changing it, but so too are many lay people for whom the ordained are the privileged authorities over the liturgical life of the church. The model thus blurs the distinction between the necessary qualities for liturgical leadership that the church has a right to expect of its clergy, and a kind of entitlement that gives complete authority over the liturgy to the clergy as soon as they are ordained. This perspective is often fostered, in spite of the best of intentions, in the seminary communities in which future clergy are trained. There, surrounded almost entirely by others who are seeking ordination or are themselves ordained, a student can almost unconsciously be confirmed in a clerical model of leadership. Once out of seminary and ordained, the new deacon or priest may find this model further confirmed by the expectations of the laity, whose own views have been shaped by years of experience with this type of ordained leadership in their parishes.

A transformed vision of ministry in the church that encompasses the diversity of ministries shared among the laity and a clarity as to which gifts are linked to ordination can only emerge as laity and clergy together grow into a deeper sense of what it means to be the church. The ministry that we should expect of the ordained is a leadership exercised within the context of a firm grounding in the ecclesial foundations of worship as the corporate prayer of the *whole* people of God.

Although the term "presider" may seem new, it is in fact the oldest term in the Christian vocabulary for one who serves as the liturgical overseer at a celebration of the eucharist. As the word implies, in the early church the person who usually filled that role was the local bishop, the *episcopos* or "overseer" of the local Christian community. This use of the word "presider," found in a document written by Justin Martyr in the middle of the second century, describes why someone with pastoral oversight for the community would also preside at the community's eucharist.[1] In other words, presiding at the eucharist was not a self-contained or limited role, but a responsibility resting upon the person whose gifts for pastoral oversight had led the community to elect him as their chief shepherd. The one who proclaimed the Great Thanksgiving over the bread and wine was the same person who gave a personal focus to the life of the community and, through apostolic ordination, signified continuity between this community and earlier generations of Christian believers, as well as with other Christian communities both near and far.

〜 The Church Made Visible

If the word "presider" bears such significance in the ancient understanding of the relation between pastoral care and sacramental celebration, to whom does the word "celebrant" belong? Through this shift of vocabulary we find that "celebrant" is a much more inclusive term than we formerly thought; it is an appropriate designation for each member of the assembly. *All* the people who have gathered are the concelebrants of the liturgical action. Thus the celebration of the eucharist is not an act of the ordained clergy that laity are permitted to observe, but the "work of the people," which is the classic definition of the word *leitourgia*. Distinctions of role are certainly found within that shared identity, but the presider does not dominate nor usurp the other roles of the various ministers, either lay or ordained. All of these ministries are complementary. Thus the only adequate response to the question of who celebrates is that the entire assembly together are the celebrants.

In this sense, it is the assembly of the local church that represents the universal church. As baptized Christians it is impossible for us to experience our membership in the church as a whole; we live always in a particular place, and our participation in Christian worship is always unique. We worship as members of a particular community, sometimes for many decades. Because we also live in a highly mobile society, however, some of us may also share in the worship life of various communities and be called to differing ministries and forms of service in each. But in all cases, we participate in the church universal through the life of one or more particular communities. When that community gathers, it is an icon of the whole church.

The assembly of a local community of Christians is thus far more than a gathering of individuals to fulfill some type of personal "Sunday obligation." The whole is far more than a total of its individual parts: in this gathering the church itself is made visible. The Sunday assembly of Christians in their various communities around the world is, for people of faith, the privileged place of encounter with the presence of God. We are the body of Christ, and each one of us is through baptism "another Christ," as the ancient terminology identified each new Christian. Our gathering is not primarily a matter of function but rather of identity: the whole body of the baptized constitutes itself in diverse communities around the world. As each one of us has been baptized into the death and resurrection of Jesus, when we assemble to celebrate in the eucharist the memorial of what God has done through Christ for the world, our identity as the body of Christ is renewed and deepened through the word and sacrament that we share. In the act of corporate worship, our union with God and with each other in Christ is revealed and strengthened.

This corporate act of faith is not centered upon itself, as some kind of nourishment of private religious sentiments. From this gathering we are always sent forth to be other Christs in the world, to fulfill our baptismal identity in building up our common humanity and immersing ourselves in service to the world, according to our particular gifts. Worship leads to service, not to personal piety. The authentic piety of the Christian tradition is always corporate; it always involves us with each other, so that we are sent out not as isolated individuals but as members of a community committed to the building up of peace and justice in our world.

～ The Assembly of the People of God

In spite of decades of liturgical renewal, we Anglicans have not paid enough attention to the central place held by the assembly in scripture and the Christian tradition. Even though we acknowledge that the laity actively participate in the celebration of the liturgy, often this amounts to little more than a change of liturgical style on Sunday morning. Such practices as the involvement of laity as lectors or chalice bearers and an increased sense of the congregation's active speaking role at various points in the service are important developments, but they remain essentially on the surface. Many lay people still see themselves primarily as listeners and observers in worship. As we come to understand how the eucharistic celebration is the action of the whole gathered community, however, we will have to make significant changes in how the liturgical action will unfold and how the diverse roles within the assembly will be exercised.

If we are to reclaim this larger understanding of the assembly as celebrants of the liturgy, it may be useful to look at the biblical and theological sources for this recovery. First, in looking at the New Testament, we learn that our word "assembly" is a translation of the Greek word *ecclesia*, which has its source in the earlier understanding of *qahal* among the Hebrew people. In Hebrew *qahal* signifies God's initiative in calling forth a people, so that the assembly of the people and its unity are a response to God's call. The fact that New Testament writers chose the Greek word *ecclesia* as their name for the Christian assembly reflects this Jewish heritage, since it had already appeared in the Greek translation of the Hebrew Septuagint. But the term was also used in secular Greek society with reference to the unity of the people of a city state. So from its beginnings *ecclesia* carried a religious and a secular connotation, both reflecting unity and the sharing of a common life.

In the New Testament *ecclesia* first refers to the local community of Christians in the city of Jerusalem, but eventually it came to mean the whole body of believers in Christ in all places. Thus in scripture *ecclesia* is the church, both the local and the universal assembly of those who acknowledge that Jesus is the Christ. If we consider the book of Acts, for example, we find both uses of the term *ecclesia*. In speaking of the time spent by Barnabas and Saul in Antioch, we read that "for an entire year they met with the church *(ecclesia)* and taught a great many people" (11:26). Here clearly is a use of *ecclesia* in reference to the local community. Later, in Paul's farewell to the elders at Ephesus, he says to them that they should "keep watch over yourselves and over all the flock, of which the Holy Spirit has made you overseers, to shepherd the church *(ecclesia)* of God that he obtained with the blood of his own Son" (20:28). Here we see the word used in its twofold meaning: in speaking of the care that the elders must show toward the local community of which they are the leaders, Paul refers at the same time to the universal church of God "obtained with the blood of his own Son."

At the Second Vatican Council, Roman Catholic bishops authorized a document, *The Constitution on the Liturgy*, which holds that "the principal manifestation of the Church consists in the full, active participation of all God's holy people in the same liturgical celebrations, especially in the same eucharist, in one prayer, at one altar, at which the bishop presides, surrounded by his college of priests and by his ministers."[2] Note the strong emphasis here on the *corporate* nature of the liturgical action of the people. This is far more than a gathering of a group of individuals for a common purpose: the fundamental nature of the liturgy is to be a corporate action *by the assembly.* Obviously this complete icon of the local church is not evident in every liturgical celebration; the bishop cannot be present at every local assembly. But it reminds us of the period in the earliest centuries when, as a small and persecuted minority, a whole body of baptized Christians were able to gather with their bishop, often with the utmost secrecy for reasons of safety. We saw this in the writing of Justin Martyr, where the bishop is designated as "the one who presides over the community" and a close relationship exists between presiding and the general pastoral oversight of the community. This model offers to us a theological point of reference for our more complex situation today. Although the bishop is not usually present, he or she is *represented* by the local parish priest so that even the smallest mission church continues to be a manifestation of the universal church.

These local assemblies are always christological—that is, they are places of encounter with the living Christ, who taught us that "where two or three are gathered in my name, I am there among them" (Matthew 18:20). The gathered community, united in Christ through baptism, is joined with Christ in praise and thanksgiving to God, which is the basis of all liturgical prayer in Christian tradition. All prayer is offered to God, through Christ, in the Holy Spirit. The public prayer of the church—its official prayer, as contrasted with the freedom that individual Christians enjoy in private prayer—is always grounded in its trinitarian faith. This does not mean that the role of the liturgy is didactic, a tool for teaching the faith, for that would distort its purpose of praise and thanksgiving to God for all the mighty acts of God from creation on through human history. Instead, Christian doctrine is the foundation for the prayer of a community already grounded in the faith professed in the poetic forms of the liturgical rite, such as the creed and the eucharistic prayer. It is in this perspective that we see the importance of the familiar axiom of the relation of prayer and belief: *lex orandi, lex credendi* ("the law of prayer constitutes the law of faith"). The church's liturgical prayer grows out of the soil of its shared faith, not as a theological lecture but as an outburst of thanksgiving and praise. Thus we might call the liturgical prayer of the assembly a self-realization of the church as a community of faith.

In addition to its christological character, the assembly also has an ecclesiological significance as the people of God. Through baptism we are formed into one body: "you are a chosen race, a royal priesthood, a holy nation, God's own people, in order that you may proclaim the mighty acts of him who called you out of darkness into his marvelous light" (1 Peter 2:9). It is the privileged role of the liturgy to be the place where, in the presence of the whole assembly, "the mighty acts" of God are proclaimed and celebrated through both the Holy Scriptures and the sermon, and in the gathering of all the members of the community at the Lord's table. All this is dazzlingly explicit in the forms of human nurture, of food and drink, now transfigured by the word of prayer to be for us the Body and Blood of Christ.

Yet that phrase referring to the consecrated bread and wine of communion, "the Body and Blood of Christ," deserves our attention. In recent decades theologians have recovered the original context in which "the Body of Christ" first emerged in Christian vocabulary. Originally it referred to the church: all baptized members who assembled every Sunday to hear the proclamation of the word of God and to share in the sacred meal. Augustine of Hippo saw these gifts of bread and wine as a kind of mirror to the assembly of their own identity as the body of Christ:

> If you are the body of Christ and his members, your mystery has been placed on the Lord's table, you receive your mystery. You reply "Amen" to that which you are, and by replying you consent. For you hear "The Body of Christ," and you reply "Amen." Be a member of the body of Christ so that your "Amen" may be true.... Be what you see, and receive what you are.[3]

Members of the body of Christ affirmed their baptismal identity in the sharing of sacred gifts that also began to be called "the Body and Blood of Christ." Over time this derived meaning came to dominate, and eventually the sense of the people themselves as the body of Christ was lost as the consecrated elements came to assume that meaning instead. Of course this contributed greatly to the enhancement of the role of the priest in the eucharist and his isolation from the gathered laity, since it was he who assumed a unique responsibility for the consecration of these sacred gifts that the laity rarely received.

The baptismal ecclesiology that we have presented is directly linked to a recovery of a sense of the Christian community as "the body of Christ." Christ is present from the time that the people assemble, as they gather in his name. This claim of Christ's presence in the assembly, based upon the words attributed to Jesus in Matthew 18:20, has a significance we have begun only tentatively to reclaim. When seen as part of a baptismal ecclesiology, it is an extraordinary assertion about the real presence of Christ in the assembly. This insight, it seems to me, comes out of a vigorous baptismal ecclesiology and should guard against a self-centered eucharistic piety focused only upon the sacred gifts. It reminds us that we are called into the world to *be* the Body we receive. This is clearly the teaching of Augustine: in a most radical way, word and sacrament in the eucharist remind us who we are as the body of Christ.

∾ Christian Initiation

By their very nature, the liturgical services of the church are never private functions. Yet in spite of more than twenty years of living with the baptismal ecclesiology embodied in the 1979 *Book of Common Prayer,* areas of the church's pastoral life still seem to lack this principle of the corporate nature of all liturgical acts. The area in which this theology seems to struggle most for a secure footing is in relationship to the rite of Holy Baptism. In most Episcopal parishes today the celebration of the baptismal rite will usually take place during, as the prayer book requires, "the chief service on a Sunday or other feast" (BCP 298). In other words, it takes place at a liturgy at which a large representation of the local community will be present. The intention behind this rubrical norm is theological: Holy Baptism is a rite of the church, not a semi-private ceremony at which a baby is "done." What is *done* in baptism is the incorporation of a person into the full ecclesial life of the body of Christ. Can this be validly done if only a few persons are present? Yes, of course. But this minimal representation of the community is appropriate only by way of exception, as in the case of an emergency baptism.

We must remember that concerns about validity always come down on the side of minimalism: what minimum is necessary for this rite to be valid or authentic even if performed under extreme circumstances? For example: "How little water may be used if a full-sized tub or basin is not available?" Or, "Which words must be said for a baptism to take place?" Yet the question of validity ought not to be merely a question of how much of the baptismal liturgy must be said, but also of how evident it is that this rite is indeed an act of the church. In an extreme situation, a dying man might ask the one other person there with him to baptize him before he died and the church would recognize the baptism's validity. However, dire situations like these cannot be used to justify celebrations of baptism at which only a very small, select number of people are present. Clearly, the frequent celebration of private rites in the past eventually distorted the theological understanding of the meaning of baptism in the minds of people generally. It does no good to insist that the theology of the rite is still corporate if, in practice, that theology has been eroded by meeting only the minimum requirements.

For example, just a few years ago I noticed that a popular church periodical was doing a special issue on baptism. Yet on the cover was a photograph that spoke volumes: it showed a total of six adults plus an infant taking part in the baptismal celebration. There was a priest vested in surplice and stole, holding a small infant in his arms, with the other adults standing nearby, all of them forming a circle around a small baptismal font that evidently held only a small amount of water. If a picture is worth a thousand words, the photograph on the cover of that magazine contradicted any baptismal theology that might be set forth in the printed articles, suggesting a whole theology of Christian baptism that is at odds with the norms authorized by *The Book of Common Prayer*. There is no sign that anyone else was there: clearly, the baptism was not taking place at "the chief service on a Sunday or other feast," and the presence of others in the community was not important. Likewise, there is no indication that the rite was taking place during a celebration of the eucharist, again contrary to prayer book norms. That such a picture, with perhaps the best of intentions on the part of the editors, should appear on the cover of an issue devoted to baptism is a rather strong indication that we still have a long way to go in shaping a liturgical mentality that is true to the prayer book's theology.

Yet just celebrating Holy Baptism during the main Sunday eucharist does not in itself assure us that a corporate sense of its meaning has actually been achieved in the local community. I sometimes find myself at a Sunday celebration of the eucharist at which a baptism is scheduled to take place, and realize that the candidate, parents, and godparents have only a distant relationship to the gathered community. Sometimes the entire group is unknown to the parish. Then the baptism is no more than a ritual element inserted into the Sunday liturgy, with the expectation that the congregation will make promises on behalf of the candidate that never can be fulfilled.

Recovering the integrity of the rites of Christian initiation is not a narrow liturgical matter needing the adjustment of a few external details. Sacramental integrity rests upon *pastoral* integrity: the sacramental rites do not stand alone but require a larger pastoral context to support and nourish them. The decline and eventual collapse of the catechumenate in the fifth to sixth centuries was perhaps the most detrimental pastoral loss in the evolution of Christian worship. As we noted in chapter one, this program of formation for baptism, often extending over a three-year period, was the means by which the church prepared candidates to make a verbal profession of faith and to undergo a complex initiatory pattern, including the water rite, anointing with the laying on of hands, and the first reception of communion.

Yet in a wider perspective, the catechumenate was an opportunity for the members of the local church to observe whether the lives of the catechumens were being reshaped into a lifestyle that accorded with the commitment of faith they were preparing to make when the time for baptism arrived. There was no rush to baptism; instead, the rite presumed that an important transformation and change of values was taking place in the life of each person who prepared for the ritual profession of faith. And so time was taken to foster this transformation. For the candidates, the catechumenate offered the context in which a reordering of their personal lives might take place. The incorporation of these new catechumens also had a significant impact on those who were already baptized, as new gifts were brought into the life of the community.

This mutuality between the community and a newly baptized member continues today. The baptism of an infant is not so much the church doing something *to* or *for* the child as it is the celebration of the miracle of their life, and the incorporation of another person created in the image of God into the body of Christ. This incorporation has a mutual effect. Through the promises, it is not only the parents and godparents who have particular responsibility for the care and nurture of the child, but the whole community gathered who, as witnesses, promise to "do all in your power to support this person in her life in Christ" (BCP 303). Yet at the same time, the newly baptized bring their own uniqueness as children of God into the life of the community. They have special gifts that cannot even be discerned at the time of birth, but which are affirmed by the congregation when they pray in the baptismal litany that the candidate may be sent forth "into the world in witness to your love" (BCP 306). In the baptismal rite a confident commitment is made, by the community on behalf of infant candidates, that their life is already marked by a vocation from God. The particular gifts of that child, at every stage of its growth, are to be supported by the community and will bear fruit within it. What is being expressed here is far more than merely the performance of a perfunctory rite with a few people in a corner of the church building on a Saturday afternoon: it is the enactment of the ongoing life of the members of the church as they seek to lead lives in accordance with their baptismal profession of faith.

∿ Encountering the Sacred

All these gifts of the Holy Spirit are needed for the building up of the common life, and all are called forth in service by the society in which we live. This understanding of ourselves as the instruments of the work of the Holy Spirit in our communities and in our world, united with the theology that each baptized Christian is "another Christ," leads us to a transformed sense of the sacred. Many of us grew up with a form of piety in which the sacred was to be found inside the church building, where we prayed in private, unbothered by the noise of the world. The Sunday liturgy was a time when a large gathering of people could, as individuals, fulfill their own personal piety needs, with other people intruding as little as possible. This was, and still is for some people, the reason behind an eight o'clock service: a gathering of people for a common purpose but to fulfill individual needs. Obviously, from a pastoral perspective, this piety must be treated gently and with respect; those who have gone before us have fostered it with the best of intentions. If the liturgy was primarily the action of the priest, why should not the laity be permitted to accomplish their own goals?

The imperative for a transformed sense of the sacred confronts us, however, when we begin to take seriously the idea that the people with whom we gather are temples of the Holy Spirit—as am I!—and that these people are, each one of them, another Christ—as am I! Thus my attitude toward them requires of me a new sense of the sacred. In this regard, the space in which God's people gather to *do* the sacred actions has great influence upon what they understand themselves to be *doing,* and upon their sense of their own sacred character as the people of God. In a seminal work on church architecture, the English priest-architect Peter Hammond wrote that his concern with church buildings was primarily regarding their significance

> as a house for corporate worship; as the place where the holy people of God meet to *do* certain things which are known collectively as liturgy and which centre upon the eucharistic action. It can hardly be too strongly emphasized that the only good reason for building a church is to provide a shelter for a worshipping community.[4]

For some, this idea of the holiness of the people who gather may seem strange. Only *God* is sacred; God is other. Human life is sinful and messy, so how can a gathering of flawed human beings be an assembly of holy people? Yet Jesus identified himself with this humanity of ours. Through his humanity we are called in our humanity into the glory of God, and in our public assemblies for worship we are given a foretaste of that glorified humanity to which we are called.

Many years ago, after the celebration of a liturgy at which many small children were present, a seminarian remarked to me that although he appreciated the fact that the children were involved in the liturgy very deeply, he missed a sense of the sacred. In his comment he clearly (if unconsciously) equated the sober and serious focus of our adult liturgies with his experience of God. I heard this comment with great surprise, since for me children so often incarnate the sense of awe and wonder that I believe to be a part of what Jesus meant when he told us that we must become like little children. Surely entering the kingdom of God will bring forth from us, at whatever age, profound levels of awe and wonder. In liturgies with children in which I have participated over the years, I have found again and again that the children bring to the assembly qualities that adult members have lost and need to recover, especially a sense of the immediacy of God. Their noise and movement break the artificiality of our "sacred silence" and oblige us to remember that we must receive the kingdom of heaven like a little child. This is not a sentimental platitude, but bedrock theology. It reminds us, as Jesus clearly taught, that we meet and serve him in other persons—those in need, those in prison, those who are hungry, and those who are young, small, and vulnerable. The assembly of Christians is not an association we must learn to put up with: it offers us the most profound and tactile experience of an encounter with God.

Discussing how we encounter the sacred obliges us, as we have seen, to consider the impact of the space in which our liturgical celebrations take place. For many people, a magnificent church building (particularly a dark Gothic cathedral) can communicate a profound experience of the sacred, even without the presence of other people. But how do we interpret such an experience? One interpretation would be the idea of the temple at Jerusalem, a shrine for the Holy of Holies, a sacred space to which only the leaders of the religious community may gain access while others remain at a distance. Certainly that mentality explains the awe many of us feel when we enter a magnificent building. But for the Christian community, I would suggest, that meaning is secondary because "the most powerful experience of the sacred is found in the celebration and the persons celebrating."[5] That is why we need to remember that it is not only in great buildings that we are able to sense the sacred, but also in simple country churches. What we often fail to recognize is that these places are holy because the people of God have over time met in them again and again to carry out the sacred actions of Christian faith. It is the people and their liturgical rites that have sanctified the space and made it holy.

This truth was brought vividly home for me many years ago when I was on a visit to England. While doing some research at Cambridge University, I decided to pay a return visit to Ely Cathedral a few miles away, a building that had impressed me deeply several years earlier. The cathedral was commemorating its nine-hundredth anniversary. It happened that I was completely alone in the building on the day of my visit, so in one sense the people of God were not there. As I walked around the outside of the choir area, I looked through to the high altar, and I realized that a new marble inlay had been placed in the area immediately in front of the altar. I presumed it would have something to do with the anniversary, and I walked over and read: "Here stood the shrine of Etheldreda, Saint and Queen, who founded this House A. D. 673." I stood there in total awe. Christians had worshiped

on that spot for over four hundred years *before* the
present cathedral was built. Suddenly I felt over-
whelmed by a sense of how, generation after generation, through baptism and marriage, the burial of the
dead, all the pastoral ministries of the church, the
round of daily prayer and weekly eucharist, this place
had been sanctified—had literally become a sacred
place—by the gathering of God's people for over thir-
teen centuries to do the sacred actions of our common
faith.

To recognize this primacy of the people and their
faith obliges us to shift from an understanding of the
church building as a shrine to one of the church building as the place of assembly. The implications of such
a shift are far-reaching. The church building is a place
of gathering where people come not as isolated individuals to fulfill the needs of private piety, but to join
with the other people of God and find once again that
God is with them to nourish them in word and sacrament and send them forth to serve the world in God's
name.

If a church building has this purpose, then some
hard questions follow. For example, does the floor
plan of the church building reflect the image of a baptismal community? Does the layout of the space support the shared experience of a gathered community?
Are the people who gather able to be present to each
other, or does the arrangement of the chairs or pews
discourage any contact with others? Does the space
reflect a clergy-dominant model of the church, with
the primary focus upon the priest in the pulpit or at
the altar and with the congregation all facing him or
her? This may seem a strange question, but if the
architecture is such that the laity are located in distant
pews and separated by altar rails, and lined up in
rows like printing upon a page and thus obliged to

remain in an observer status, then that building will suffocate any reenvisioning of the community as a baptismal church. No matter what is being taught, the primary assembly on Sunday has a formative impact on that community's self-understanding. If the building contradicts the teaching, as Bishop J. A. T. Robinson said many years ago, "The building will always win—unless and until we can make it say something else."[6]

Many of our buildings date from a period when an understanding of the church as the assembly of the baptized was significantly obscured, and those buildings weigh heavily upon us, especially with their clear separation between the place where the clergy and official participants perform their ministries and the pews in which the people sit. The cost of tearing such buildings down in order to build new ones that might better foster the common worship of the assembly would be enormous, but we cannot ignore the impact of the space upon the people who gather there. In recent years a number of architects have shown a remarkable gift for taking a clergy-dominant model building and reenvisioning it, sometimes in very modest ways, so that it more adequately reflects the assembly's proper image. With the passage of successive weeks and years, a church building so reordered promotes a renewed self-understanding for all who gather there for worship. The building does have powerful impact on the actions that take place within it.

～ The Foundation of Ministry

Underneath all of this chapter lies a foundational question: What is the basis of ministry—baptism or ordination? The church has long assumed that the ordained exercise ministry in some primary way that the laity do not, no matter how dedicated and self-sacrificial their service may be. Yet surely experience and reflection within the church during recent decades has shown us that *all* forms of ministry are a response to a call that emerges from our baptismal covenant. The clerical model saw ministry as "by the few for the many"—the "many" being the laity. Yet a baptismal ecclesiology suggests that ministry is "by the many for the whole," and that these diverse ministries take many forms according to the realities and gifts of our various communities. Such an understanding of the nature of the church rests upon the conviction that gifts for oversight and service—the charisms of Paul's epistles—are given by the Holy Spirit in great abundance, and all are needed for the fulfillment of the church's mission in the world.

It is from this perspective that we need to see the significance of the restoration of the classical catechumenate in many parts of the Episcopal Church in recent decades. The goal of the catechumenate is far greater than that of the confirmation classes through which many of us joined the Episcopal Church. Formation in the fullest sense is the real issue: not merely to know something about church history and how to find our way through *The Book of Common Prayer,* but to become rooted in the Christian faith and devote our particular gifts to the service and care of others, especially the destitute of our world. Such formation leads to an understanding of "full participation in the liturgy," which is far more than saying the responses and singing the hymns. Listening to the reading of scripture at the liturgy together with other believers becomes a weekly occasion to hear the great story of salvation history and to unite to it our own personal story in thanksgiving for God's gracious presence in our own lives, as in the lives of our ancestors in faith who have gone before us. The linking of our own story to the great story of salvation is central to the purpose and meaning of our assemblies as God's people. Full participation worthy of the name is a dynamic engagement with the words and signs of the liturgy, recognizing that in them we find the promise and assurance of an abundant life in God.

Chapter Three

Whose Culture?

Liturgy in a Multicultural Church

In the 1970s I agreed to address a joint meeting of the clergy of a midwestern Roman Catholic diocese and the corresponding diocese of the Episcopal Church. In a wonderful atmosphere of mutual affirmation among the clergy gathered that day we explored two emerging areas of convergence, namely, the eucharist and holy orders (the ordained ministries of the church). At the conference a Roman Catholic priest asked me, "Why do you always refer to us as *Roman* Catholics? We do not refer to you Episcopalians as Canterburians." His question was put humorously, but I decided to answer him in a substantive way.

Christian communities, I explained, are always grounded in time and place—in his case, the papal organization of his tradition links Roman Catholics in a direct way to the city of Rome. Similarly for Anglicans, there is a primacy of honor attached to the Archbishop of Canterbury and thus, regarding origins, to the English (or Anglican) Church with its own particular history. The church's identity is always explicit and local, never merely theoretical or abstract. To say that I am a Roman Catholic or a Lutheran or an Episcopalian indicates more than merely the name of the particular tradition in which I worship. Inherent to these names is a geographical association that, at least historically, has had a formative impact. In other words, the dominant characteristics of our traditions were shaped within specific cultural contexts. The geographical association of Rome or Augsburg or Canterbury with these three traditions carries the wider implication of how people living within a particular historical and cultural context have had their experience and understanding of Christian faith shaped by it.

Hidden beneath our discussion that day was, I now believe, the issue of *culture*. Our two traditions are embedded in two different cultural frameworks—factors that are far more significant than we recognized at that time. We realized that our separate histories and theological traditions often expressed understandings that, we were coming to see, were complementary rather than opposed. Yet it was also clear that the evolution of our separate traditions had unfolded within two different patterns of religious experience.

A person cannot be a Christian "in general." We are baptized in a specific place at a specific time, so that although we are by baptism members of the universal church, our membership is always experienced within a specific ecclesial context, in a specific parish or mission church made up of a particular group of people. We will live out this membership within the social and cultural realities of one particular community or many different communities over the course of a lifetime. Our forebears may well have lived their entire lives within one such community; today such stability is far less common. Many Christians are aware from their own experience how socially and culturally different our various congregations are, and how these differences are reflected in diverse patterns of liturgical prayer.

My first experiences as an ordained priest were in Latin America, where I quickly learned that although the communities I served were members of the Anglican Communion, their patterns of prayer, especially in common devotions practiced at home, did not correspond to the ethos of an American congregation. I particularly noted the much more common use of the rosary in private prayer, and the cultural celebrations attached to certain popular saints' days. The hymns and sacred songs used in these contexts were also drawn from resources, both evangelical and catholic, that were not typical of Anglican hymnody.

There is, in fact, no way to participate in the Christian tradition except within the framework of some particular cultural, historical, and geographical whole. Christian faith is always incarnate and always reflects the fundamental doctrine of Christianity that in Jesus God has participated in our human reality. By implication it follows that God participates in the whole of our human diversity, not merely in one cultural pattern. Christian faith and practice is more than theoretical; our theory—our theologizing—about that faith and practice is always after the fact. Christian theology reflects on the experience of actual Christians in the living of their faith. This is expressed in corporate worship and in the ordering of their daily lives in accordance with the imperatives emerging from the common life shared by the members of the body of Christ. Christian faith is always grounded in a shared social and cultural context.

～ The Separation of Sacred and Secular

Alongside the clerical model of the church we considered earlier, with its emphasis on uniformity and conformity, is a widely held presumption that Christianity is a *trans-cultural* religion. In this view the Christian church is seen as a universal culture that simply holds together certain aspects of the particular culture in which it is planted, transcending what is local and particular except for accidental factors such as language, local custom, or musical materials that a liturgical rite requires. Even with regard to these, there is a tendency to hang on to those elements that at an earlier time expressed a living but distinct culture. This has been characteristic of all the various liturgical traditions in one way or another.

In the Roman Catholic tradition, for example, preserving Latin as the virtually universal liturgical language was a clear expression of this trans-cultural quality. Similarly, among Anglicans there has been a strong impulse to maintain, with as little modification as possible, the liturgical language shaped by Archbishop Thomas Cranmer in the sixteenth century. When I was confirmed in the Episcopal Church in the 1950s, the use of these archaic English forms, admittedly beautiful to the ear, was justified on the grounds that it kept liturgical language distinct from ordinary English (not to mention ordinary American!) and thus hallowed the sacred context in which it was used. Clearly, the maintenance of Latin among Roman Catholics and "Elizabethan English" among Anglicans were both expressions of a trans-cultural understanding of the church's liturgical life. The implication was that for this holy use in the liturgy, the language of corporate prayer had to be different from the language of ordinary daily life.

The perspective of history, however, deals a lethal blow to this argument. The gradual introduction of Latin in the Roman Christian community from about the middle of the third century reflects the fact that

Latin had emerged to replace Greek as the primary *everyday* language of the society. Had a trans-cultural mentality been in force at that time, Greek would have remained the language of liturgy precisely because it had *ceased* to be the everyday language of the people. Instead, just as in the Reformation of the sixteenth century, the church shifted to ordinary language because it was convinced that when the Christian community gathers for the celebration of the liturgy, it should be done in a language understood by the people.

Yet the idea that liturgy should embody a trans-cultural understanding of this central activity of the church's life was expressed in other ways, too. The language question is merely one aspect of a much larger pattern of factors in the church's life which, I believe, are rooted in the clerical understanding of the church. For clerical authorities, the ritual actions they celebrated—such as the eucharistic meal—bore less and less resemblance to their natural human parallels. This attitude grew out of a particular understanding of the Holy defined as utterly "other"—as absolutely unlike anything we ordinarily know. The fact that all of the sacraments bore relation to comparable actions in human life became obscured. Thus, for example, the eucharist as a ritual meal came to manifest little correspondence with what we as human beings experience as a meal, as a shared human event in which we eat, drink, and are nourished.[1]

In a clericalized model of the church it was possible for the eucharist to be a sacred meal at which no one but the priest would eat and drink, bearing little resemblance to the abundant agape meals of the early church. Similarly, the rite was not celebrated at a holy table comparable to the dining table in a home, but at a shrine-like sideboard that had become a throne for the adoration of the eucharistic elements. What had originally been eating and drinking in a way that united us to the meals Jesus shared with his followers became instead a remote sacred talisman with which the people might "communicate" through their eyes in an act of adoration. In the rite of baptism, likewise, by the Middle Ages the cleansing waters of the baptismal bath and the rubbing of the body with fragrant oil had been reduced to the sprinkling of a few drops of water and the making of a cross on the forehead with a smidgen of oil.

There was no subversive intent behind these shifts. Their effect, however, was to obscure the natural symbolic sense of bread and wine, oil and water, and to imply a highly abstract understanding of the symbols in order to safeguard the otherness of the sacred. These changes, furthermore, took place within a culture—a specific social, historical, and cultural context—that saw the priest alone as essential. The role of the priest as presider of the assembly at the eucharist became one in which he alone was needed for the liturgical action. Consequently the understanding of the eucharist that held sway during the first several centuries of Christianity became radically eroded as the people ceased to experience the liturgy as the shared action of the whole gathered community.

This clericalized understanding of the liturgy was by no means authentically trans-cultural, for that is an impossible ideal. Instead, it reveals how the medieval church took on social patterns that were derived from the larger society. The alienation of the laity from the clergy emerged from the realities of a highly stratified feudal society in which social class had the final word. For the laity at the bottom of the social scale, this meant in practical terms illiteracy and an almost total absence of catechetical formation.

Together with the common theological perception that human unworthiness and sinfulness were barriers to receiving the sacred gifts of communion, it virtually guaranteed that the laity were profoundly alienated from any role in the church's worship other than that of a bystander.

Pastorally speaking, Holy Communion offered an occasion for repentance, and the rite of reconciliation as preparation for communion was canonically regulated as an annual event that took place at Easter. Consequently, as a result of this defection from the sacramental norm of regular communion, the majority of the laity were left to assume that their eucharistic obligation was fulfilled in attendance and in looking upon the consecrated loaf of bread and chalice of wine when they were elevated during the eucharistic prayer. It is not my purpose to trace the historical evolution of the eucharist from sacred meal to focus of adoration, which is well documented elsewhere.[2] What is important for us here is to recognize that this alienating form of sacramental encounter was theologically justified by an appeal to the awesome holiness of the rites. All aspects of these sacramental rites were prescribed by and restricted to the priest, a person officially sanctified through ordination and anointing. Like the sacred gifts, the ordained priest was thus set apart from the ordinary into the distinct category of the sacred. The result was the creation of a set of rituals that, by language and content, had little relationship to the social rituals of ordinary daily life. The medieval liturgical edifice, entirely controlled by canon law and enacted by the clergy, assumed an otherworldly holiness as a sacred culture complete within itself, untainted by the blemishes of the world. For a time, the church rested securely enclosed within what it claimed as its own world.

As distant as we are today from the period in which this evolution occurred, it is not appropriate for us to stand in judgment on the choices made at that time with regard to the church's sacramental life. It is quite possible that given the roughness of the social fabric in the ninth and tenth centuries, this alienation of the sacred from the secular might have seemed the only way possible for the church's leaders to safeguard the sacred actions entrusted to them. There had developed such a sense of the "otherness" of divine realities—including, of course, the consecrated bread and wine of the eucharist—that the clergy had a special obligation to protect them from any taint through contact with ordinary sinful humanity. A priest's hands might touch the holy objects because they had been anointed and thus made holy in ordination. Similarly, on those rare occasions when the laity came to communion, the consecrated host was placed directly into their mouths rather than in their unconsecrated hands.[3]

Furthermore, historical knowledge about the far different liturgical theology and practice of the early centuries of Christianity, known to us today through the recovery of early documents, was not available to medieval scholars of the time. Yet if we should not be harshly critical of this deterioration of sacramental practice because of the problematic nature of the social context, nevertheless we can insist that this sacramental edifice of the medieval church does not offer us an eternal paradigm appropriate for all times and places in the church's life.

Nonetheless, its impact is with us still. Society at large is indifferent to the internal workings of the church's life, yet within our various Christian communities the effects of this separation still shape the sacramental understanding and expectations of many

Christians. The idea persists that for something to be sacred it must be radically distinct from the secular. In this context, liturgical piety is like a highly cultivated hot-house plant flourishing in its own private world. The liturgy is seen as a "place" into which a devout person can escape from the storms and stresses of secular life.

Needless to say, this type of liturgical piety has been strongly resistant to the liturgical changes of recent decades, which are often interpreted as intrusions of the world into the sacred realm. For people formed in this piety, liturgical change seems a betrayal of their experience of God, a violation of their sense of the sacred. This betrayal comes in a variety of forms: in revised liturgical books using contemporary language; in services where laity have a high degree of involvement; in the introduction of less formal, seemingly casual, patterns of worship; and in the idea that pastoral discretion might allow a departure from the printed text in certain situations. Perhaps what appears most dangerous of all is the idea that a congregation might even need to develop new rites for use in situations where a ritual is needed but no liturgical forms have been authorized. In my own experience such pastoral situations have arisen with regard to the miscarriage of a child, for example, and in the context of the dissolution of a marriage in which both members were asking for God's blessing upon them as they continued forward from the failure of divorce into new and now separate paths.

∾ Liturgy and Local Culture

During recent decades, such adjustments in our public worship have been a response to authentic pastoral imperatives. One of the most significant adjustments in our liturgical rites has been the rapid assimilation of inclusive language texts. When the question first arose regarding the preparation of texts acknowledging that our congregations are made up of both men and women, I was serving on the Standing Liturgical Commission. Our initial authorization from the General Convention was to prepare inclusive language texts based upon the rites already contained in the 1979 *Book of Common Prayer*. Thus as we began our work, the members of the commission attempted to make minimal adjustments to the rites of Morning and Evening Prayer and the Holy Eucharist by such methods as changing masculine pronouns to plural (and thus, we thought, inclusive) pronouns. We soon realized that this method produced maimed rites in which the flow of the language of the original texts was undermined by minor and irritating alterations. We came to the conclusion that the rites of the 1979 prayer book should stand as they were, and that what was needed were *new* texts that would be developed from within a framework of inclusive language.

The first focus of our work was to address inclusive language regarding the congregation—in other words, to shape texts that would acknowledge that people of both sexes were gathered. The 1979 *Book of Common Prayer* had already made some advancement beyond its predecessors in this regard, but much more was needed if the new texts were to be fully inclusive. Coming out of this initial work in the mid-eighties has been a series of rites authorized for experimental use. This is still a project in process, but it is an explicit example of how a liturgical rite that takes into account the reality of the gathered community can be prepared only by people gifted with an awareness and sensitivity that can embrace the wide diversities found in our society.[4]

Another aspect of inclusive language concerns our liturgical language about God. For most of the history of Christianity, authority and power in Christian societies have been attributed to the male, and that male dominance has shaped a liturgical language in which references to God's authority and power have been cast in male images.[5] Certainly many images of God in scripture are male, but there are also female images of God as, for example, a mother who would gather her young. In our work on the Standing Liturgical Commission, we realized that there was a rich tradition of metaphors about God, both male and female, and from the whole creation, which had been gradually whittled down in the tradition of official texts to the overwhelming benefit of the male images. Those images, in turn, had profoundly shaped the faith of worshipers with regard to their understanding of God.

The work of the commission regarding language thus went far beyond merely tinkering with the words of the liturgy. Reinterpreting the part that the liturgy plays in the Christian life changes all our priorities. We move from a clerical preoccupation with rubrics and ritual details to a view in which the whole liturgical tradition and the authorized texts are seen as the primary resource for the community's public prayer. Yet it is a resource that must be enfleshed in the lived realities of the community's life. That is why the question of *culture* suddenly emerges as a primary factor in the shaping of the norms for a community's public prayer. Unlike a ritual model imposed from above, in an ecclesial model the fundamental structures of Christian corporate prayer take flesh—yes, *are incarnate*—through the local community's life. Whereas a trans-cultural model was presumed to fit any and all situations because of its "universal" character, models grounded in the local culture become the nexus, the meeting point between that local community in its life and faith and the great tradition of the church's worship.

This issue is one of great importance for the liturgical traditions of all Christian denominations. All of them have, to one degree or another, been affected by the culture of the clerical model. Whenever a religious tradition has officially authorized texts and rites, it has been the task of the clergy to conform to them and thus to implement their binding character. The fact that this ideal was seldom fully realized did not diminish the impact of the principle that an authorized liturgical text was intended for the use of all. Furthermore, any practices or innovations that a parish priest might introduce tended to be dictated by the priest's personal piety rather than by the pastoral needs of a particular community. This might be seen particularly in the sometimes bizarre hand gesture routines some priests perform during the Great Thanksgiving: the multiple signs of the cross and other movements can seem more as the manipulation of the bread and wine than their consecration. When I have had occasion to question clergy who practice such routines why they do them and what they mean, I have been told simply that "that is the way I learned to do it before my ordination." And it appears that little further thought has been given to the matter after that. Since the consecration was seen as a kind of deep personal act by the priest, there was no awareness that one might need some self-scrutiny for the often confusing gestures that the people are expected to observe. A person who presides at a public action—whether sacred or secular—needs to be aware of the impact of their body language upon those who have gathered.

For Anglicans, strict adherence to an authorized rite can, when transferred to non-Anglo cultural contexts, end in liturgical absurdity. When I began my ordained ministry in the Diocese of Puerto Rico I was quite naive about the significance of the cultural differences between the United States and my new home. Although the local congregations were made up of Latin Americans with a sprinkling of North Americans, it was a perhaps unconscious assumption that as a diocese of the Episcopal Church, the parishes and missions would, as much as possible, adopt the religious culture of the United States. This became clear to me during my first year when I saw a copy of a newly published hymnal in Spanish for use in the Hispanic dioceses of the Episcopal Church. The hymns and the liturgical music for the eucharist and the offices were, on the whole, simply adapted versions of materials from the American hymnal. In other words, there had been little effort to incorporate music that was representative of the local culture, with the result that the majority of the hymns were poorly adapted versions of English-language hymns. This was liturgically absurd because music functions within the liturgy as an expression of the ethos and gifts of the people who have gathered to pray.

Gradually it dawned upon me that as a missionary priest from the United States I was not only a representative of North American Anglicanism, but also an agent of North American culture and values. I was aided in discerning this problem by sensitive Puerto Ricans, many of whom were not active in any of the Christian denominations that proliferated around the island. To one degree or another, these various denominations reflected the cultural character and priorities of the nations from which their missionaries came—and the majority were from the United States.

Without any conscious intention on my part, I was implementing an Anglican variation of the trans-cultural understanding of liturgical worship. Likewise, in spite of its long history of missionary work in Latin America, the clergy of the Roman Church were cultural missionaries as much as I was, except that they were bearers of the cultures of Ireland and Spain. In spite of its long presence, the Roman tradition had failed to take root within the culture. Roman Catholic friends constantly lamented to me that there were very few local vocations either to the priesthood or to the religious orders, with the result that parishes tended to be staffed by clergy imported from abroad where there was an abundant supply, and similarly the religious communities were made up primarily of foreigners like myself.

The significance of all this burst upon me quite early in my ordained ministry. In January of 1962, I was scheduled to officiate for the first time at a wedding. Although by that time my spoken Spanish had reached an acceptable level of competence, as I rehearsed the texts of the marriage rite by myself, I realized that the language was strangely archaic, even artificial in its idiom. In working with these texts, it dawned upon me that at the wedding I would be using a non-idiomatic Spanish translation of the marriage rite in the 1928 American prayer book—which was itself a modestly revised version of the English rite of 1662! That rite, in turn, was deeply indebted to its medieval antecedent and consequently to the medieval social world in which it first developed. For example, it implied that the young woman who was to be married was the property of her father up until the time she was transferred to the possession of the groom.[6] I felt myself to be in a cultural time warp.

The medieval English rite, I realized, was completely external to the culture of the Latin American community in which it was being celebrated. It was "trans-cultural" in the worst sense of the word. Local people accepted this situation because they, too, had been conditioned to think of the church's rituals as expressions of that "other" sacred world through which the sacraments were conveyed. Such rites were a kind of sacred veneer spread across the underlying human reality.

It was no wonder, then, that the local communities often embodied the human reality of their own culture in family rituals they held at the times of birth, marriage, and death as a supplement to the church's official rites. For example, it was the custom in Puerto Rico for the godparents (and *not* the parents) to take the child to be baptized. When the godparents then returned the child to its parents, there was a ritual dialogue that had developed locally in which the newly baptized child was welcomed home now as a Christian. The mother would say to the godmother, "I gave you a pagan, and you have brought me a Christian." It was through such local customs that the meaning of the sacramental rites was brought into the personal faith life of the people.

I began to discern cultural tension in other aspects of the church's life. The North American "packaging" of the tradition was particularly evident in the design and appointments of several new parish buildings which were built in the 1960s in Puerto Rico as part of a general expansion of Anglicanism in Latin America. When I visited these buildings, I recognized that they might easily have been constructed in almost any part of the United States! Since we were serving local communities of modest size in Puerto Rico, we were not building in the imitation-Gothic style found in large American cities for cathedral or major parish congregations. Yet the principle was very much the same. The design of the buildings reflected a theoretical ideal—that is, what a church building *ought* to look like—based upon North American models. There was no thought that the local churches might reflect the culture of the people who would gather in them.

Not surprisingly, the appointments in these buildings—the pews and hymnboards and other artifacts—were often chosen from the catalogues of church supply houses in the United States. It was as though these external aspects of North American identity were not translatable into the artifacts of the local culture. In contrast, I often saw in commercial buildings being built in the cities of Puerto Rico beautiful work produced by local artists in glass, wood, and wrought iron, and felt an enormous sense of regret.

The authorized liturgical books we used were similarly out of step. Both the prayer book and the Spanish hymnal reproduced as nearly as possible the design and layout of these same books in the United States. The implication was that these authorized versions of the official books of the Episcopal Church were the authoritative models for worship in the Hispanic dioceses of Latin America. Far more serious, however, were the editorial principles governing the translations, which continued as normative throughout the 1970s. Translations of the prayer book into Spanish and French (for use in Haiti) would exactly correspond, item by item and phrase by phrase, to the materials in the American authorized version. This policy made of that book the equivalent of an *editio typica* imposed by Roman Catholic authorities as the absolute norm for translations throughout the world. Translation meant "transliteration": versions of the text that do not respect the integrity of the second language because of an excessive fidelity to the authority of the first.

Although the dioceses of the Anglican Communion in Latin America have now moved beyond this textual rigidity, their earlier experiences still furnish an important lesson in how reluctant a dominant culture is to bestow autonomy on younger ecclesial communities. This reluctance reflects the intensity of the belief held by the dominant culture that its own norms possess a sacred aura that makes them adaptable to any cultural context. But that, of course, is precisely the problem.

⌒ Prayer Book English

What is required for the authentic flowering of Christian faith in different cultures is not adaptation, but what is called "inculturation." This word implies more than a veneer from the local culture applied to a set of presumed trans-cultural rites. It means that the underlying intentions of the tradition of Christian worship are to take form, flesh, and structure within the particular cultural realities in which a liturgy will be celebrated. The liturgy of a local church appropriately reflects its own indigenous culture. A locally designed vestment—though well meaning—can often be mere tokenism, because it is the fundamental dimensions of Christian faith and practice that must be incarnated in the deepest structures of a society's culture. Otherwise it is difficult to see how that faith and practice are to be claimed as its own. In areas of the world that were evangelized in the eighteenth and nineteenth centuries, often the imported culture eventually is seen as a foreign export imposed from beyond through domination; thus the Christian faith itself becomes an aspect of foreign domination rather than God's message of good news to all humanity.

For the Anglican tradition, this cultural issue is particularly important and problematic. Unlike the Lutheran liturgical tradition, which quickly flowered in diverse cultural and linguistic contexts during the century following the Reformation, the worship tradition of the English church remained wedded to English as its liturgical language. One might speculate how different the religious history of Ireland might have been if Queen Elizabeth I had approved the translation of the 1559 prayer book into Gaelic rather than insisting on its use in English. This imperialism for the sake of bolstering political and religious conformity meant that the Irish people had the choice of two foreign languages for their public worship: Latin or English. Furthermore, the imposition of the English liturgy upon the Irish was a potent expression of the political domination that has plagued relations between Ireland and England for centuries. In the end such imperialism never achieves its goal, as we have seen in the enduring conflicts in northern Ireland where the hostilities nurtured in the sixteenth and seventeenth centuries remain unresolved.

The powerful link between the prayer book tradition and its use of English was also fostered, admittedly, by the remarkable quality of the texts prepared by Archbishop Thomas Cranmer and later imitators. The influence of these texts upon the larger scope of English usage can hardly be overestimated. "Prayer book English" established itself as a hallowed liturgical language, much as Latin had at an earlier time throughout the western church. The use of the language of worship produces over time a kind of lapidary quality, polished through prayer from generation to generation. In a similar way, musical settings of such texts, as they become established through regular use in liturgical celebrations, begin to signify a whole community's experience of the sacred.

Finally, one other factor in the universal use of prayer book English in worship outside the Latin tradition was that the first century of the history of the prayer book coincided with the emergence of England as the most powerful nation on earth. Because of England's powerful political and economic engagements all over the world, English Christians carried their forms of worship with them to every corner of the globe. Local peoples were expected to learn the language of their rulers. English missionaries often used trade routes or paths of politically extended influence to preach the gospel of Christ, carrying *The Book of Common Prayer* with them. This meant that even as the faith was proclaimed in other cultures, the English of the prayer book still retained a kind of primacy. Only gradually did translations into local languages appear as the church expanded among people for whom English was unknown—and even then, as in India and Africa, English often remained the common language in areas inhabited by diverse linguistic groups.

All of these factors contributed to the remarkable tenacity of Cranmer's liturgical English as the prayer language of Anglican Christians. This also explains why the imperatives of our own multicultural world are such a profound challenge to Anglican identity. There are those today who feel that Anglicanism is so marked by its English cultural and linguistic identity that it lacks the flexibility to adapt to the extreme cultural complexity of the modern world. Even to attempt such a transformation, it is argued, would rob the tradition of its essential cultural identity. We must also remember that even today there are clergy in England who reject the idea of an "Anglican Communion" because for them the English church is precisely and *only* that, the church of the English nation. Thus the multicultural character of contemporary society is even more problematic for some English Anglicans than for Anglicans in other parts of the world. Even allowing for the imprint of English culture upon the liturgical heritage of Episcopalians, in the United States we are accustomed to the image of the melting pot and its influence on our national identity, at least from the nineteenth century onward. But in England today there is serious question as to whether Christianity itself (not merely its Anglican form) will be the religion of a majority of the people in a few decades' time. At present the number of people who adhere to the Islamic faith is substantial in Great Britain: it is said that those of Islamic faith in England who gather on Fridays for worship are in number comparable to the total number of Christians who gather on Sunday. One would be foolish to claim a kind of Christian primacy in such a transformed cultural context. Thus even in the historical roots of English religious culture the question of cultural pluralism cannot be avoided.

∽ The Question of Beauty

Any discussion of the cultural adaptation of the liturgy must confront the complex question of how we are to understand and define "beauty" in a particular cultural context. Beauty has a profound link with the experience of the sacred. This is no superficial identification of the experience of the Holy with aesthetic experience, nor an assertion that all Christians make a direct connection between the experience of beauty and their faith in God. The danger in even raising the issue of beauty is that it may seem to imply an identification of religious experience with matters of "good taste." My intention is to pose this question at a much deeper level.

In liturgical acts, meaning is always expressed through the senses. In other words, our liturgical worship of God always involves us in the use of external means—candles, crosses, clothing—that embody the meaning of the ritual action for us. Our use of such externals implies that they support the primary intention of liturgical prayer, which is to express our shared baptismal faith. When these externals do not support that intention, then they should be abandoned. For example, at times in the history of Christianity an excessively elaborate liturgy—what one Anglican theologian referred to as "meretricious gaudiness"—has led some Christians to be suspicious of externals in worship on the grounds that they hint at idolatry. The Puritans in England were critical of *The Book of Common Prayer* for just this reason. Rather than supporting the community's act of faith in worship, the rites with their explicit expectation of absolute conformity (as imposed by law) seemed to get in the way and distract the community from the primary purpose for which they had gathered. The liturgical rites of the prayer book were merely the *forms* of prayer rather than authentic prayer itself. We should not be naive about this danger. All of the liturgical churches have, at one time or another, had to confront the problem of *ritualism*, that is, an excessive preoccupation with ritual priorities. As distinct from good ritual, which is intended to embody and support the prayer of a people, ritualism makes the ritual an end in itself, in which the purpose of public worship is understood as the exact *performance* of the authorized words and actions.[7]

Because of our physical nature, we human beings express meaning through our bodies, through external acts such as words, gestures, and movement. If we love another person, that love is embodied in words, actions, and, often, in some material gift. To give a loved one a gift on a birthday, for example, is not the love itself, but it embodies that love in ways that are tangible for the beloved. Indeed, it is hard to imagine how love can be known and received without such external expressions. Although the cost of a gift is not essential to its value as a sign of love, yet as the giver we seem always to want that gift to be the best we can give.

I believe that this aspect of our humanity offers an insight into the meaning of liturgical worship. As a lover will use words and gifts to embody and express love for another, so the church, made up of physical human beings, gathers to express its love for God in a shared act of faith. The goal of our liturgical rites is always to embody and express authentic faith. And since these acts are by their nature external, we are always obliged to make choices with regard to the form and design these external expressions will take. So, although the people of God may gather in any adequate space for worship, the character and quality of that space profoundly influence our experience of the action within it. The same applies to all the elements of our worship. We may read scripture from any edition available, but when we hear the word of God proclaimed from a place of honor, by a vested minister, and perhaps surrounded by burning candles, it is all these elements together that communicate to us the importance of what is taking place, and the significance we give to it. In such a context, for the reader to proclaim the word from a tattered little paperback or a bulletin leaflet does not change the words that are said, but it deeply affects how we perceive their importance. The externals *do* have their impact upon us.

This is simply to say that the criteria for beauty play an important role in the external dimensions of liturgical prayer. Human beings are nourished by beauty: we feel awe at the sight of a majestic mountain, we take delight in holding a well-crafted vase or pot, or we are moved by the sound of a chorale by Bach. A fact of human experience is that our senses draw us into a world of sensual delight. This experience is a kind of nourishment for our souls just as important as food for our bodies. From this perspective, the importance of beauty for the life of faith is perfectly clear. My own first experience of the beauty of the liturgy was on Easter Day in 1950 when, as a Jewish teenager, I was taken by a Quaker teacher to attend the principal Easter service in the National Cathedral in Washington, D.C. I do not remember what the preacher said or any of the details of the rite; what I remember is the beautiful space, splendid music, and the vast assembly of people gathered to praise God. It was the first time I saw the link between beauty and the worship of God.

In 1970, Russian novelist Alexander Solzhenitsyn was awarded the Nobel Prize for literature. In his response to the award, Solzhenitsyn quoted a phrase from Dostoevsky: "Beauty will save the world."[8] He said that although truth and goodness can be perverted from their true purpose, beauty remains sovereign, elusive, unpredictable, and free. Beauty does not take the place of the good and the true, but is their indispensable companion. Without beauty, goodness and truth tend to become frozen into narrow intellectual systems that betray their own highest intentions.

Can we say, then, that beauty has a role to play in God's plan of salvation? This insight was affirmed by the great leader of the Oxford Movement, Edward Pusey, in the nineteenth century. At his own expense, Pusey subsidized the building of beautiful churches in the impoverished urban areas of England. In the sermon he preached at the consecration of one of these churches, he said that his purpose was to bring Christian worship in its beauty into the lives of people who were starved for any experience of beauty in their daily lives. Pusey's gift enabled them to worship God "in the beauty of holiness."

Why speak of beauty in a chapter on culture and the need for the church to embrace the cultural diversity of our world? The reason is simple, and it relates to the trans-cultural model I discussed earlier. One aspect of that model is its prescription of clerical norms for virtually every aspect of liturgical worship. These norms tend to include a very specific pattern of aesthetic priorities. A good example of this is the often unconscious assumption that Gothic architecture is somehow the most appropriate for places of worship: because of that assumption, Anglican missionaries built Gothic cathedrals in Asia and Africa. In other words, they built worship spaces that reflected the liturgical, musical and architectural ideals of the high Middle Ages, which they saw as the great age of faith; they were acting on the assumption that these ideals were normative for all times and places.[9] Clearly, this view encased its understanding of sacred beauty within a narrow cultural and historical framework.

The challenge of our multicultural world, however, obliges us to recognize that although beauty remains an important aspect of Christian worship, decisions about what *is* beautiful cannot be so easily made. With regard to the aesthetic side of worship, the norms of what is beautiful must be related to the culture of the people who gather. Those norms cannot be imposed from outside: they emerge from among a people as they are permitted and encouraged to use their own cultural forms to express the faith in God, who in the Incarnation embraced all the cultures of the world. We gather in all parts of that world with a common need to be spiritually nourished by word and sacrament. Yet in addition to that universal need that all Christians share, we are culturally diverse, and gather within a specific cultural and social context. So the character of our worship carries both a commonality with all other Christians and also the particularity of our own society. Our enactment of the liturgy must embrace these two dimensions and permit "the beauty of holiness" to be embodied in meaningful forms of beauty for the people gathered.

～ Cultural Diversity in Anglicanism

Can the tradition we know as "Anglicanism" embrace the rich cultural pluralism of our world? The very word itself may contribute to our difficulties with cultural diversity simply because of its strong implied link with British history and tradition. Many of us would take the hopeful view that Anglicanism is a form of Christian faith and practice that can take root and flourish in the widely divergent cultures of the modern world. Perhaps we have arrived at a time when even the term "Anglicanism" is not an appropriate designation for our communion of sister churches. The Church in Japan recognized this long ago when it constituted itself as the NIPPON SEI KO KAI, the Holy Catholic Church of Japan.

The fundamental characteristics of the Anglican tradition, setting aside for a moment a range of influences arising from the English ethos, are quite clear and offer a vigorous model of Christian faith and practice. We could begin with the statement known as the Chicago-Lambeth Quadrilateral, which expresses those dimensions of the Church Catholic to which Anglicanism has given consistent witness (BCP 876-878). This document was developed as a ground plan for the healing of the divisions among Christian traditions, but its Anglican origin suggests its value as a reference point for those characteristics that are held to be essential in our tradition: the Holy Scriptures as the rule and standard of faith; the Apostles' and Nicene creeds as the statement of Christian faith; the sacraments of baptism and eucharist as ordained by Christ; and the historic episcopate, locally adapted "to the varying needs of the nations and persons called of God into the Unity of His Church."

We find nothing in these four fundamentals that is narrowly linked to English history or culture. Rather, these are universal characteristics for a universal church; they offer a basic structure that can flourish in any of the world's cultures. The fourth characteristic—the historic episcopate—is, even in the Quadrilateral itself, singled out as subject to local adaptation. In other words, even the historic episcopate cannot be preserved as an absolute form to which various cultures must adjust. Instead the opposite is true: each culture must shape the principle of apostolic continuity in terms of its own cultural identity. Although the writers who crafted the Quadrilateral could not have foreseen the extraordinary cultural pluralism of our time, their wording offers us a much-needed principle upon which we may base our own work today. We are living at a time when the traditional liturgical forms must take new flesh in a world characterized by dazzling cultural diversity.

Even the hallowed and tradition-bound office of the papacy is being reexamined, as John Paul II has invited Christians outside the Roman Catholic Church to explore how the papacy needs reformation to better serve the church of the twenty-first century.[10] In effect, this is an invitation with significant multicultural implications not only for Roman Catholics but for all the Christian traditions. It implies that our heritage of cultural domination must now give way to a new vision in which the hope for Christian unity is genuinely inclusive at every level of the church's life. We are coming to recognize the inhibiting effects of this domination in the evangelization of the many world cultures other than our own.

No list of characteristics written in the past, either in the early centuries of Christianity or a mere century ago, can be absolute or definitive for the church today. We are living at a time when new imperatives face the church, when the pastoral realities are complex, and when formulations and rituals from past generations can at best offer us a point of reference as we seek to respond from the resources of Christian faith. We all wish to hold to continuity with the previous generations of the church, back to its origins in Jesus Christ. Yet continuity itself is not static; it is not merely an adherence to models from the past. The challenges of inculturation oblige us to find authentic continuity within change. The characteristics of our Anglican heritage that we most cherish will live into the future of the church not as fossils of the past but through their *incarnation* in the widely diverse cultures of our world.

The massive defection from Christian practice we see all around us is a clear sign that the trans-cultural models of the past are in fact culturally and historically bound to the past and perceived as irrelevant by most people in our world. With perhaps the best of intentions, missionaries to Asia and Africa carried with them not merely the faith of the church but also the specific cultural expressions of that faith from their own homeland. As was noted earlier, this led them to the construction of Gothic style churches in cultures in which such buildings were profoundly alien, and to the implementation of English models of liturgical prayer which put a stranglehold upon the development of indigenous rites among the Anglican and other liturgical communities in Africa. The message those missionaries brought was that the faith and its outer forms were of one piece. Even more damagingly, they suggested that the local culture could not offer appropriate forms in which the Christian faith could be expressed because that culture (not to mention its indigenous religious forms) was dismissed as pagan and thus inferior to their own. Only in recent decades have the churches of Africa begun to develop their own liturgical forms that both link them to the great tradition of Christianity and are expressive of their own particular cultural heritage.[11]

There should be no doubt that the perspective offered here requires a radical and wrenching renewal of the church's life. Yet it is an imperative if the spiritual values of the tradition of faith in which we have been nurtured are to take root within a dramatically different world. It serves no purpose now for us to impugn the understanding of culture held by those missionaries of the preceding centuries who carried the Christian faith to every corner of the world. Yet the consequences of identifying the faith they proclaimed with the culture from which they came have created crippling inhibitions upon the church in our time that make it difficult to proclaim that faith in terms that have any significance for a large number of people. Our lived reality is a post-Christian world; our culture is no longer that of western European medieval Catholicism, nor are we ruled by anointed kings. In other words, the *world* in which the gospel is to take flesh is utterly different from that in which Christianity exercised cultural and social dominance. We should not lament that change, but see it as a gift and challenge from God to us as we seek how we may live and proclaim our faith in what is still God's world.

Chapter Four

Whose Music?

The Arts as Embodied Prayer

In a southern city where I had been giving a program for the diocese, I decided to stay over for the weekend and attend the eucharist simply as an ordinary visitor. Hoping not to be recognized as a professional liturgist, I decided not to wear a clerical collar. I have found over the years that I can learn a great deal about the worship and life of a parish simply by dropping in, and that morning I learned a lot.

I arrived early for the principal service and sat in my chair for several minutes, quieting myself to prepare for the liturgy. A few minutes before the scheduled time of service, the organ burst out with an extraordinary expression of joy. If I had not already known it, the music alone would have reminded me that we were in the season of Easter. Aside from the sheer beauty of the music, it also communicated to all of us gathered there that something very important was taking place. When the prelude ended, we were already in a state of expectancy—and that morning, the liturgy did not let us down. The acolytes and crucifer were waiting at the back of the church, and the organist introduced the opening hymn with phrases woven around the familiar theme. We were brought to our feet to lift our voices in a great hymn of praise. The people of God had gathered.

"Music in Christian worship is an embodied form of praying," the distinguished Methodist liturgist Don Saliers has noted. "Liturgy is inherently musical."[1] If Saliers is correct, then the significant role of music in Christian worship is not to be understood as an ideal for special occasions, but as a normal and integral part of the liturgy. Yet this normative place of music in our liturgical assemblies is not found in the typical church-going experience of many Christians. When music does play an important role in the liturgical life of cathedrals or large parishes, the model is often that of performance: musicians supply the music accompanying the rite while the congregation listens. Quite frequently the musical participation of the laity is restricted to the singing of hymns, which are used as "filler" rather than as musical settings of texts that are an essential part of the liturgical whole. And even when music is seen as an integral part of the liturgy, Christians differ widely on the *place* of music in liturgical celebrations—running the whole range from professional performance to devout participation.

Music is a major aspect of a society's culture, whether it be music that people perform themselves in halls, homes, and churches, or music that is heard in concerts and recitals or recorded electronically by professional musicians. However, I have decided to discuss the place of music in worship in a separate chapter from that on culture because, as Don Saliers claims, music is the preeminent art in liturgical celebrations. The nonverbal emotional power of music (whether or not words are involved) lifts the worshiping community into a different realm, so that our worship becomes a sensual engagement with the Holy

One. Music thus embodies with particular power the church's theology of Incarnation.

Liturgy in its fullest sense does not merely give us information about the ways of God, but embraces all that we are as human beings and invites us to bring our whole bodily selves into an encounter with the living God. That is how music in worship links our emotional selves, the whole feeling side of our humanity, to the ongoing renewal of faith that liturgy both expresses and nourishes. As a people of the Incarnation, we must never attempt to put aside our sensual selves in order to engage God only with our minds. Among the strongest spiritual principles of classical Anglicanism is its insistence that the life of faith requires an intimate union of heart and mind, each serving to illuminate the other.

Music sung by a congregation, furthermore, has a remarkable power to bring us together and remind us that Christian worship is never a private or individual activity. Even when I pray alone in my room, I pray as a member of the people of God. Music in liturgy nourishes that conviction even more, building up in us a sense of our unity, what the New Testament calls our *koinonia*, our fellowship in the body of Christ. It is in the liturgical assembly of God's people that we are physically constituted as the risen body of Christ in our world, not merely individuals gathered for a common purpose. Music in worship contributes strongly to our shared experience of the liturgy as a prayer-action in which we participate as a community of faith.

In recent years a substantial number of writings have appeared that address the role of music in Christian worship. Not surprisingly, their authors reflect differing approaches even within the context of those Christian traditions whose public worship is characterized as "liturgical"—that is, churches whose music is structurally related to a pattern of authorized ritual texts. In such writings, furthermore, one often finds hints of the frustration that exists because of the gap between the theoretical claim about the essentially musical character of the liturgy and the reality that in many churches music is seen as decorative and inessential. For the latter, the liturgy is primarily an authorized collection of words and texts. If music is used at all, it is limited to a small repertory of familiar hymns. In cathedral churches and large parishes having the financial resources for a music program, all too often this music is simply performed for a listening public. As beautiful as such music may be, it is more appropriate to a concert hall than to a liturgical rite.

Questions regarding the role of music in the liturgy are very complex. My intention here is to focus on these questions in the light of the recovery of a baptismal ecclesiology that is the recurring theme of this book. Our understanding of the church shapes our expectations when we go to attend a liturgical celebration. We shall consider some ways that liturgical music and liturgical structure have intersected in the past to both expand and limit the possibilities of the role that music might fulfill. And we will look at some of the ways that music in liturgical prayer can mirror and incarnate the cultural diversity of our congregations. Clearly, just as we must move beyond the clerical model of liturgy, so we also must renew our sense of the place that music should occupy in corporate worship.

Such renewal, it seems to me, is imperative for the pastoral, liturgical, and musical leadership in all Christian communions. The alternative would be to try to hold on to an earlier model of the church as fixed in a particular time and culture, such as the model of medieval Christendom in a world which, as we have observed, no longer exists, but which many have tried to maintain as an ideal model for all times and places. It is foolish to try to revive this model that no longer nourishes the faith of countless Christians who are trying to live out their Christian commitment in terms of the realities of our world. A theology of the Incarnation requires nothing less.

⌐ Expanding Our Musical Horizons

What criteria would we have to use in order to expand our musical horizons in this way? For criteria are required if we are to avoid giving the impression that *any* music may be helpfully used in the liturgy: just as we choose our *words* in the liturgy carefully because they must fit and fulfill their intended purpose, so our choices in music must be made thoughtfully and with a view toward the whole. If, as I believe, music is integral to liturgical prayer, we need criteria that respect, first of all, the craft of music—whatever style it is in. This means that, to the fullest degree possible, the musical leaders in our various communities would have both musical and liturgical training.

It may seem strange to speak of liturgical training in this context, but the fact is that in many of our congregations it is not uncommon for parish musicians to do their work in virtual isolation from liturgical planning. In the past, general liturgical planning itself was often comparatively rare, but even with our abundance of worship committees a comprehensive consideration of the way worship is done in a given congregation is not all that common. In many parishes, once a model has been established for Sunday worship, clergy tend simply to stick to it, adapting it to the special circumstances of any given Sunday.

Consequently, churches with a large musical program tend to adhere to a performance model that fits in well with the expectations of parish musicians. In smaller parishes and missions with modest resources, on the other hand, music in the liturgy is often limited to the insertion of hymns at certain fixed points in the service, such as prior to the reading of the gospel or at the offertory. Far too often there is no attempt to select hymns that would illuminate the theological or pastoral implications of a particular feast day or liturgical celebration; instead, they are often viewed merely as "filler." And yet it is a marvelous experience to take part in a liturgy in which the hymns have been chosen with attention not only to the season but also to the scripture readings. Hymnody can serve as a significant extension of the impact of the proclamation of the word of God.[2]

Not too many decades in the past, both clergy and laity of the Episcopal Church understood the liturgy as entirely at the discretion of the clergy. This was a canonically enforced expression of the clerical mentality that we considered earlier. Musicians were generally not expected to have any explicit liturgical training or formation. That is one reason why the renewal of the liturgy associated with the preparation and implementation of the 1979 *Book of Common Prayer* burdened the community of church musicians in unexpected ways. Many musicians were simply unprepared for the musical imperatives that emerged from within the new liturgical context of the prayer book. Under such circumstances it is hardly surprising that conflicts surfaced, and continue today. Frequently the work of liturgical planners and musicians who now try harder to work together is impaired by the fact that they are operating from two very different liturgical models.

The criteria generally accepted today as the basis for shaping the role of music within a liturgical celebration are *musical, liturgical,* and *pastoral.* All three criteria flesh out the cultural imperatives that open up the horizon for what might be significant change in the role of music in the liturgy.[3]

~ The Musical Criterion: Is it Well-Crafted?

The musical criterion is concerned simply that musical craft be respected and that music in the liturgy, whatever its style, be well composed. Badly crafted music, as seen especially in the notoriously sentimental harmonizations of some eucharistic settings and many hymns, is simply not worthy of inclusion in Christian worship. This sounds like an elitist point of view, and obviously, if not linked to the other priorities, could very well reinforce the familiar performance model that we are seeking to discard. The conviction behind it, however, is that inferior music is unworthy of Christian prayer. Such a criterion does not imply that we limit our music for worship to what has generally been considered in our various traditions as the "sacred style" of liturgical music—whether plainsong, Tudor motets, or polyphony. The aim is not to restrict musical style, but rather to make sure that the music is a worthwhile example of the musician's art, as well as an authentic expression of the musician's culture.

There is no question that in the service of the liturgy some of the most glorious music ever written has been added to the musical treasury of the world. In our own tradition of Christian worship, the repertory of settings of the texts of the Holy Eucharist; of the canticles, psalms, and other sacred texts; of religious poetry; and even of specifically theological writings is

vast beyond imagination. Anglicanism has been widely eclectic in the range of music that has been used in
the context of the liturgy.

We are the beneficiaries of a great body of material for Morning and Evening Prayer and for settings of
the Mass from the pens of such Tudor composers as
William Byrd, Thomas Tallis, and other composers
associated with the tradition of English polyphony.
We have also been given great anthems from that
period, as well as the choral works of George Frederick
Handel and his contemporaries. There is likewise a
rich body of musical resources for the daily office and
eucharistic liturgies from nineteenth-century composers such as Charles Stanford and Hubert Parry,
and from twentieth-century giants such as Benjamin
Britten and Ralph Vaughan Williams. The Catholic
Revival in the nineteenth century, under the influence
of the Oxford and Cambridge Movements, reintro-
duced plainsong both in settings for the offices and the
eucharist and in hymns translated for use in the
English liturgy by John Mason Neale and others.

On the whole, none of this music was aimed at performance by the people in the pew. Generally it
required rehearsal and a high level of professional
training, and rested on the assumption that most of
the music of the liturgy would be performed by a
choir. Yet even more important than the questions of
what type of music was used and of choir performance versus congregational participation is the question of the liturgical mentality that much of this
music embodies: for what kind of liturgical celebration is this music intended?

By the criteria of musical craft, one would say that
most of this large repertory, with its wide range of
styles, meets the standard of well-crafted music, and
much of it is great music. However, there is also a

body of music that eventually fell into disuse because of its poor craftsmanship. This poor music might include musical settings that do not respect the sense, rhythm, and phrasing of the text. Another familiar characteristic of poor quality liturgical music is the use of harmonic settings that are maudlin and tend to trivialize the text. In some churches, inferior music has been inflicted on worshipers for generations, convincing them that when the word "sacred" precedes the word "music," they can expect a sentimental, badly crafted result. A steady diet of such music, similar to the effects of too much candy, will rot the spiritual teeth of a people and shape a sweet and sentimental piety that is inadequate for the challenges of the Christian life. It presents a serious pastoral issue.

The temptation is to look for easy solutions, but there is no quick fix. In many ways, the real question is a larger one: a performance mentality regarding the music of the liturgy that goes hand-in-hand with a clerical mentality regarding the liturgy as a whole. If this underlying issue is not confronted seriously, then the question of whether the music is of good or poor quality becomes insignificant, since the fundamental nature of the liturgy as the action of the whole people of God remains misunderstood.

Obviously, once this larger question of the basic understanding of liturgical actions has been studied and discussed, then the issue of poor quality music arises within the spectrum of choices about what music will be used in a specific community. But a new vision of the liturgical action means that much of the former repertory, both good and bad, will not fit the liturgical structure. Some music may be appropriately used as choir anthems or as music for the concert hall. But, as we shall observe, music developed for performance does not fit easily into models that presume the full participation of all who have gathered.

Questions about the quality of the music raise the question of musical styles. What style of music are appropriate to use in the liturgy? Many Christians who have worshiped in the more traditional styles of liturgical prayer throughout their lives continue to be well served by the treasures of the church's musical heritage. Without even thinking about it, they know that a great hymn is right for their worship because it continues to be an effective medium for their offering of praise and as an expression of their faith. Yet the spiritual power of such a hymn is often linked to a personal memory of singing it at liturgical celebrations over many years. In other words, its *familiarity* is an essential part of its effectiveness, which becomes obvious when a new hymn tune is introduced. In spite of the similarity of the style, a new hymn seldom engages our spirits at the depth that a familiar hymn can reach. It is this particular music and not merely the text that is rooted in our religious experience. Text and music form a whole. This implies that for the future, on the whole, we should encourage the creation of new texts with new musical settings, and maintain the great hymns of our heritage in their integrity. In this way, the repertory will expand.

Although after years of church-going we tend to associate certain styles of music with worship, there really is no such thing as a specifically religious style of music. After all, music is made up of specific pitches that are simply set down in a given rhythmic pattern and then "colored" by the use of particular instruments and voices. When we listen, for example, to Mozart's *Requiem*, its *religious* character is determined not by the style of the music, but by the fact that it is a funeral mass. A similar musical style will also be found in many other compositions by Mozart whose texts have nothing to do with a funeral, or with any other specifically religious or liturgical context.

In theory, I believe that *any* musical style can express religious faith. In actual practice, I have arrived at that view rather slowly; some styles, no matter how excellent the craft of the composer, have such strong secular associations that their use may always be jarring. When a liturgical text is involved, we expect the music to support and proclaim the sense of that text. Thus some of the more aggressive and even violent styles of contemporary music seem an unlikely prospect for liturgical use.

Even so, I believe that this question must be attended to with great care and that no style should be excluded without careful discernment involving those who would be using it in the context of worship. A few years ago I had an experience that obliged me to look at this issue with greater openness to diverse styles. I was in Austin, Texas, to do a program for the Roman Catholic diocese, and I was invited to attend the eucharist at the Paulist Center on the campus of the University of Texas on Sunday morning. I arrived to find a combo of nine musicians who had selected contemporary music in an idiom that I would not have chosen—it reminded me of a night club. This was a question of style, however, and since the make-up of the congregation that morning was mostly college-age Roman Catholics, I realized that this was "their" music. The liturgy planners had looked at this question very sensitively, and the music and the texts were carefully integrated into the liturgy. Contrary to my expectation, the style had been adapted effectively to a liturgical context and we did not feel we were at a performance—or at a night club!

The implications of this are potentially far-reaching. In our own culture, which is increasingly diverse, a wide variety of musical styles reflecting the different character of a specific congregation should find a place in our liturgical models, and in doing so, expand our musical horizon. Within the Episcopal Church, this should lead to a greater musical diversity than we have known up to now. For most churchgoers, even the integration of differing styles can itself be a quite new experience. In the past, the use of complete settings of the ordinary texts of the eucharist *(Kyrie, Gloria in excelsis, Credo, Sanctus-Benedictus, and Agnus Dei)* written by a single composer in a unified musical style conditioned worshipers to think of these pieces as an organic whole. The historical facts are quite different, however, and there is no inherent reason why diverse musical styles might be incorporated not only in the hymnody but also in the service music itself.

∼ The Liturgical Criterion: Does It Fit the Function?

The liturgical criterion has to do with the role of music *within* the liturgical action. Music is not merely something to be added onto the liturgy or inserted at convenient places to give the people some way to participate in the service. The liturgical criterion is a safeguard against treating the rite *only* as an occasion for the performance of great music. If the music is truly integral to the rite then we are, in fact, talking about *ritual* music, that is, music that serves and underscores the liturgical action.

The performance of sacred music can still be the occasion of a profound spiritual experience. Concerts of sacred music are widely attended by people who would never think of attending a service at a church, but find in this music, and often in great music in general, an authentic experience of the Holy. I do not undervalue the importance of this type of musical experience, but it is not the fundamental purpose of music in the liturgy. Certainly an anthem sung by the choir can fulfill both a liturgical and an aesthetic role, but music based upon the liturgical texts should never cease being accountable to those texts. The music should support their proclamatory intent.

Many years ago, a friend who is a Dominican priest went with me to a great liturgical celebration at an historic Episcopal parish. The music was glorious, but at a certain moment the underlying nature of the occasion, at least from a musical perspective, revealed itself. The critical moment came at the singing of the *Sanctus* during the eucharistic prayer. It was sung only by the choir, and the music went on and on with many repetitions of the word "Holy." Suddenly my friend sat down. Later he explained to me that when he heard the fifteenth "Holy," he realized he was no longer at a liturgy but at a concert! This is the issue with which the liturgical criterion is concerned: musical settings must not overwhelm the text, but serve it.

Much of our music for worship was written at a time of liturgical degeneracy. This may seem an excessively strong word. Yet we see the result of the deforming clerical model when we hear music intended for use with the liturgy that was written with an utter indifference to what was actually taking place in the service. It comes from a period when the rite itself belonged almost entirely to the celebrant at the altar, and the musical elements were left to the discretion of professional musicians, who saw the liturgy as the occasion for a "sacred concert." To expand our understanding of the role of music in liturgy requires that the musical aspect of liturgical worship engage the liturgical rite with more integrity and take into account the sequence and meaning of the liturgical *actions*, not just the texts.

The effect of identifying music for the liturgy with a particular sequence of *texts* can be seen most clearly in our tradition of musical forms for the eucharistic rite—the Ordinary of the Mass. We noted earlier that this union of a certain set of texts came to imply that, when sung at a particular eucharist, they would be composed by one composer in a single style. Whether we are talking about plainsong, polyphony, the music of Haydn and Mozart, or contemporary settings in diverse styles that include folk music and jazz, the issue is the same. Composers who set out to write music for use at the eucharist are inhibited by the fixed structure of the Ordinary outlined above: the *Kyrie* (Lord, have mercy); *Gloria in excelsis* (Glory be to God on high); *Credo* (the Nicene Creed); *Sanctus* (Holy, holy, holy); *Benedictus* (Blessed is he who comes in the name of the Lord); and *Agnus Dei* (Lamb of God).

This pattern of texts has, of course, a hallowed place in the history of liturgical music. But has it led contemporary musicians and liturgists into a set of assumptions that now, in our multicultural world, must be questioned? Those who have studied the historical evolution of the eucharist are aware that far from coming into the eucharistic rite as a united musical structure, each element of the traditional Ordinary has a separate and distinct history. The *Kyrie*, for example, was originally created as a response to a litany of intercession that in the fifth century was moved to the beginning of the service in order to give the ministers in the service time to make their way into the sanctuary of large churches. Such an entrance rite only became necessary when the assemblies of Christian worshipers had so increased in size—after the fourth century—that large buildings were needed as gathering places.

The *Gloria in excelsis,* on the other hand, was a hymn of praise to God that had originally been used at the morning prayers of Eastern Orthodox monks. Its inclusion in the eucharistic rite was, to say the least, rare. At first restricted to the pope's celebration of the Easter Day eucharist, the *Gloria*'s more widespread use by bishops and eventually by priests developed only very gradually. It became normative for use on appointed feast days only in the second millennium. In other words, the joining of the *Gloria* with the *Kyrie,* as we know it in our prayer book today, only came about at a rather late stage in the evolution of the eucharist. Originally these two liturgical texts had no direct relationship.

The text of the *Sanctus* was the first element to find a place within the structure of the eucharistic rite, and that place was, not surprisingly, within the primary prayer of the rite, the Great Thanksgiving. There is documentary evidence that the earliest forms of the eucharistic prayer did *not* include this great text, which links the praise of the people gathered with that of the choir of heaven, but certainly the *Sanctus* had found a place within the prayer by the fourth century.[4] The *Agnus Dei,* on the other hand, having its own distinct history, was introduced into the eucharistic rite in the seventh century to provide a musical "filler" for the period of time during which the leavened loaves were being broken up for the communion of the assembly.

Finally, we may note the completely distinct history of the *Credo.*[5] The creed sometimes strikes people as a somewhat strange interpolation into the structure of the eucharist, and this reaction is justified by history. It was inserted into the eucharist for a coronation in the eleventh century, and came only very gradually into more general use in the west. (Its use in the eastern church came about earlier—in the sixth century—in connection with the opposition of Orthodoxy to the Arian heresy.) At first it was recited only occasionally, but it gradually came into regular use on Sundays. For Anglicans, Archbishop Thomas Cranmer established a more frequent use of the Apostles' Creed by making it a fixed element in Morning and Evening Prayer, and by authorizing the use of the Nicene Creed in celebrations of the eucharist on all Sundays and feast days. Cranmer's purpose, however, seems to have been catechetical: that is, it was a way to be sure that the laity learned these texts. Given the abyss into which lay education in the faith had fallen, the regular recitation of the two creeds in the liturgy offered an opportunity for the laity to learn these and other basic texts about which, with the Latin liturgy, they had often been ignorant.

By observing that each element in what came to be called the Ordinary of the Mass has its own unique history, we begin to see that the linking of them into a united musical and liturgical whole is at best artificial. It led, as we well know, to the creation of a remarkable body of sacred music on these texts, but it was the music of the choir and not of the people as a whole. This evolution was not wrong. It is simply a fact in the history of liturgical worship: the Ordinary as we know it today evolved out of the performance model of music in worship and was delegated to a trained choir.

Further, these different parts of the Ordinary were all *musical* elements. These texts were musical parts of the liturgical rites, not words to be recited out loud. Yet most of us have attended celebrations of the eucharist at which some—and perhaps all—of these texts have been said rather than sung without anyone present feeling that something rather odd was being done. To a Christian in earlier centuries it would have been inconceivable that such musical texts should be *spoken*. Yet once these texts became fixed parts of the eucharistic liturgy, to be used with or without music, they came to be used in ways that originally were never intended. Knowing this historical background is critical for us because it informs the way we shape the liturgy today. An understanding of the original intention of a particular part of the rite—why certain texts and actions are where they are in the liturgy—gives us a basis for greater flexibility as to how music can be integrated into our worship today.

For example, there are many contexts in which parts of the traditional eucharistic liturgy—or perhaps even the rite itself—are not appropriate to a given occasion. Perhaps the musical settings of the texts found in the hymnal are not part of the local community's musical repertory, or these settings are too difficult for the congregation. Or perhaps the usual musical resources are not at hand for that occasion—the organist might be ill that Sunday, or the service might take place in a nursing home or hospital room. In such cases we should not choose between either saying the traditional texts or eliminating them, but rather should find music that fulfills the structural purpose needed.

I have often seen this problem while worshiping in parishes that do not know any musical setting of the *Gloria*. A hymn of praise is sung at the opening of the liturgy as the ministers in the service enter—and yet that hymn of praise is then followed by a spoken recitation of the *Gloria in excelsis*. It would make more sense, however, for the hymn of praise to *replace* the *Gloria* because the whole point is that music itself is the best way to express its attitude of praise. By the same token, it would never occur to anyone to *speak* the text of "Amazing Grace," and yet we do not seem to apply this same common sense to other hymnic texts as well.

Obviously, traditional musical texts like the *Kyrie* and the *Sanctus* should not be abandoned; there will always be occasions where they will continue to fulfill their musical and liturgical purpose. Their place in the liturgy is established by centuries-long use in celebrations of the eucharist all over the world. Yet even in those places where the texts of the Ordinary are always used, I hope that the *saying* of these texts will cease and that their original musical purpose will be reestablished. Hymns do not fulfill their intended liturgical role if they are *read*. We have all experienced the added dimension that the *singing* of a great hymn brings to our praise of God. The text and music become one reality. The singing of a great text is a different experience from saying it; singing lifts us into a deeper dimension of praise and the text is thereby transformed to a deeper level of significance.

～ The Pastoral Criterion: Is It Appropriate to This Community?

The final criterion for expanding our musical resources is the pastoral one. Often it has been overlooked, especially with regard to the issue of culture. Once we affirm that a particular musical composition is of good quality, and we know it is right for the context, the question remains, "Is the music right for *this* community?" As we have seen to be the case with liturgical rites, music for the liturgy has often been conceived in the limited perspective of classical western Christianity. As the church had its rites, so also it had its music. To the clergy fell the task of keeping music of poor quality out of the liturgy, so authorized documents tended to limit the approved resources to a very narrow range. But this also meant that other musical styles were seldom explored.

Yet since music is such a significant expression of culture, it is imperative that the musical horizon broaden dramatically in a multicultural world. The musical issue before us today will require creative solutions to the problem of how our music and worship can relate to the multiculturalism of the twenty-first century. In many cases, this broadening of horizons will require a radical rethinking of the ways that music can play an integral role in public worship. For example, little is achieved in the use of Hispanic music, jazz, or any of the wide range of contemporary forms, if this music is simply *performed* before the congregation.

Certain fundamental aesthetic principles have characterized Anglican worship for almost five centuries. These principles can be summed up in the phrase that has been invoked by Anglican preachers as "the beauty of holiness in the worship of the Church of England." The phrase is, of course, based upon the words in the prayer book invitatory canticle, the *Venite*, which is sung at the beginning of Morning Prayer (BCP 44-45).[6] This quality of beauty in Anglican liturgical prayer was found somewhere in between the "dryness" of Puritan worship and the "gaudiness" of Roman Catholic liturgy. It was reflected in the beauty of the liturgical language and of the music to which these words were set. In sum, beauty in Anglican worship, according to the great body of apologetical writings, was found in the balance and integration of all the diverse aspects of liturgical prayer, words and music, the bodily senses, and ritual movement.[7]

If these principles are to take flesh among Anglicans today, liturgical and musical leaders will have to do much more than merely adapt the texts and music that have served as Anglican liturgical models in the past. It is possible to envision a time when the liturgical conformity that has been characteristic of Anglicanism around the world will be replaced by a range of models whose cultural diversity will be enormous. When that happens, we will have to enlarge our understanding of how the liturgy serves as an expression of unity, since unity will no longer be based on conformity to a set of prescribed texts.[8]

It is from this starting point that the vision of music in liturgical worship must greatly expand. In terms of the Ordinary and its restraining effect upon the texts of the eucharistic rite, this new multicultural vision would require musical and liturgical leaders to shift their focus from the words to the structure: the rite's underlying dynamics of gathering, celebrating and proclaiming the word, participating in the holy meal, and dismissing. Such a structure, of course, cuts to the bone: this is the skeleton of the liturgical action. Fleshing out this structure in a wide variety of cultural contexts means understanding all the ways that a community of neighbors gathers and celebrates events, talks about God, shares meals together, and departs. In this way the liturgy would embody particular forms of ritual expression that are part of a particular community's cultural identity.

This task became clear to me through an experience in my own ministry back in the 1970s. I was invited by the bishop of Ecuador to spend time in the interior of his diocese, in the upper reaches of the Amazon River, with a group of Quetchua Indians who were members of a small Episcopal community. Among them, the bishop had discerned qualities of leadership that might lead him to ordain some of them to serve locally, either as deacons or as priests. The bishop asked me to spend time with a group of these potential ordinands to give them a basic grounding in liturgy and sacramental theology.

In our discussions about the eucharist as a sacred meal of the whole community, we discovered a problem: among the Quetchuas, men and women do not eat together. For a moment, I was up against a brick wall. How could I find a model for talking about the eucharist that connected with their culture? I asked, "Are there no occasions on which men and women eat together?" And they responded, "Only at weddings." I was delighted! Here was a wonderful way to see the eucharist—as a wedding feast between God and the whole human family. The exploration of these kinds of cultural links is an imperative for inculturating the liturgy within the widely diverse communities in which the life of the church is planted. Such inculturation requires us not to impose the traditional forms with which the Christian faith was so long identified in western European culture, but to seek out within each culture the best ways to express the meaning of the gospel.

We are talking here about *inculturation* and not merely *adaptation*. Inculturation embodies some fundamental aspect of the church's life and teaching in the forms of a culture other than that in which they have previously been known. What might that mean with regard to music in the liturgy? In the first place, we must begin by looking beyond specific texts and ask how they function within the context of a rite. What is the *function* of musical elements within the classic structure of the eucharist, which is relatively unchanged since the seventh century? In a multicultural church, what ritual music can fulfill these basic functions and at the same time use and celebrate the musical idiom of a distinctive culture? How do the different musical texts serve to gather the community, support the proclamation of the Word and the sharing of a sacred meal of bread and wine, and then send the community forth to serve in the name of Christ in the world? How can we harness music's extraordinary ability to intensify the power of words and engage the religious affections of a particular community?

Trying to fit music *around* the words of the rite, whether with traditional hymns, folk music, or popular music of the local culture, misses the point. The liturgy is not an arrangement of words or a set of texts. It is a religious and social *drama* in which a variety of elements—movement, music, gesture, word, touch, and smell—come together in what is a single action, an action grounded in faith. Not only is the mind engaged, but the whole human person—heart, mind, and physical body—participates. In this way the members of the assembly become full participants in God's renewal of grace in the lives of the people who make up the liturgical assembly.

∽ Embodied Prayer

We cannot leave the subject of music without spending some time on another musical element in the liturgy: movement, or more specifically, dance. For it is through movement, through our bodies, that we communicate with others. It is quite natural for many of us, in conversation with a friend, to express ourselves just as much in body language as we do in words. Even when our bodies are still for a time, especially in moments of intense focus or meditation, we can sense within ourselves interior movement as we enter more deeply into an awareness of the presence of God.

Given that we are physical beings, bodily movement has more significance for us than merely getting from one place to another. Movement takes on other dimensions of meaning. In all the cultures of the world, bodily movement is the way human beings celebrate an important event through processions or formal rituals. For example, after the ritual celebration of their marriage, the bride and groom are drawn to each other in a dance while family and friends join them in this expression of their joy. Dance *celebrates* the event. It is a powerful, nonverbal expression of the meaning of uniting two lives.

On major academic occasions, the entrance procession of a faculty dressed in their elaborate regalia is not merely a way to get them to their seats, but an essential rite of passage. Those who have served as teachers and mentors now share with the graduates in the commencement of a new phase in their lives. On the Fourth of July, St. Anthony's Day in Little Italy, or when our football team wins, what is more natural than a parade? And when one group is excluded from marching, it amounts to a kind of dehumanization of the excluded group. The meaning of such bodily "events" is so inbred that it would never occur to us to question whether or not such responses are appropriate. We walk together, we run together, we play together, and we march together as expressions of a shared humanity. Such common actions are perhaps second only to the sharing of food and drink together as the sign of a common life.

Where does liturgical movement fit into this picture? Certainly on great religious occasions, or even Sunday by Sunday in larger church buildings, we see the importance of bodily movement. The slow procession of liturgical leaders moving through a large cathedral or parish on Ascension Day or Pentecost, dressed in festive garments, proclaims the celebratory character of the event. Even within the rite itself, ministers, readers, and servers move back and forth as the sequence of liturgical actions unfolds. If incense is used at certain points in the rite, we have the experience of a ritual dance as the presider moves with graceful gestures around the altar, spreading the aroma of incense, or as the thurifer moves among the ministers and the assembly.

Yet generally speaking, movement in our liturgical rites is quite restricted, even inhibited. Often the sanctuary area in which the altar stands is cluttered with so much furniture and other paraphernalia that bold gestures and movements are virtually impossible. The presider and assisting ministers may be cut off from the assembly by an altar rail, which stands as a barrier between the sanctuary area and the congregation. As for the people, they are generally restricted to the pews, which keep them in orderly rows as they all look in one direction toward the presider at the altar or in the pulpit. Because of that focus on the presider, the people in the pews have no dynamic sense of themselves as a *gathered* people. Earlier I spoke of the impact of architecture and interior design upon the self-understanding of the assembly. We cannot worship over a period of years in our typical liturgical spaces without them shaping how we see ourselves as God's people gathered for corporate prayer. Our principal liturgies on Sunday, which are dominated by words and texts, were shaped with adults in mind, at a time when children were not seen as appropriate participants in the worshiping community. The adults know when to be still, to listen, and to watch while the clergy fulfill the primary ministries. But that is, of

course, the mindset a baptismal ecclesiology turns
upside down.

My experiences in worshiping with children have
led me to see them as naturally liturgical beings, precisely because they are so physically involved in what
is taking place. Unless, that is, they are being
restrained by adults. The message we adults send is
that when children can behave like us, which means
to sit quietly and to be still, then they will be welcome
at adult worship. In other words, our bodies must be
repressed before we can participate in the liturgy. But
rather than having the children learn their behavior
from adults, it might sometimes be better if we adults
learned from the children. I am not being sentimental
here: my convictions about the gifts children bring to
the liturgy are based upon a long experience of liturgies with children in which they opened my eyes to
the larger horizon of corporate prayer. They seem
quite naturally to involve their whole bodies in worship.

Perhaps it will be the children in our congregations
who can liberate us from the physically subdued way
of worshiping that has been the experience of many of
us throughout our lives. Children are so wonderfully
in their bodies. Their energy seems boundless: they
move, they play, they dance. Pews make children rest-
less. Their movements, their noise, their tendency to
wander away from the pew into the aisle and even up
into the sanctuary, have led adults to think that children simply are not "ready" to be present at adult
worship. And so children are relegated to the Sunday
school or perhaps to "children's chapel," furnished
with miniature altars, pews, candlesticks, and other
adornments found in "big church." There children are
prepared to participate in the full, adult version of

church when they have shown themselves capable of behaving properly.

Yet it is precisely children's sense of their own bodies that can be their gift to the adult community as an essential means of transforming our physically stilted ways of worshiping. The baptismal foundation of the congregation's identity I have been setting forth in this book creates an imperative for the inclusion of children—not by a forced conformity to the adult pattern, but as agents for its transformation into an authentically inclusive model and one that embraces all ages and all stages of human development. It is crucial to recognize that the process of transformation children bring to the assembly also affects its ability to be hospitable in other ways. It awakens us to the needs of a multicultural community, including those of its handicapped and elderly.

I learned a great deal about this during the last two decades of my mother's life, when she came to depend upon a walker and a wheelchair to get her around. As a deeply faithful Christian, the eucharist was at the absolute center of her life, and whatever her physical state, she expected to participate fully. In my care for her, I came to realize how insensitive we are about the needs of those who are handicapped or elderly, once we see their essential place in our liturgical assemblies. All of these people—like young children—challenge our sense of inclusivity: the church's worship should be the place where *all* are welcomed, and this cannot be merely in words on the program. Authentic hospitality must be *embodied* through an intense alertness to how our liturgical spaces can become truly places in which all may find a welcome. If we are able to realize that the inclusion of *all* the baptized is an absolute imperative, not merely an option when convenient, then the Sunday assembly will be an authentic sign of the gathering of all God's people.

The full inclusion of all people is never going to be easy. It requires attention and thoughtful adaptation of the liturgy. It obliges liturgical leaders in the parish or mission, including both lay and ordained, to prepare models of worship that are more than the unimaginative repetition of authorized texts from *The Book of Common Prayer*. The liturgical rites are *prayer*— not merely texts to be recited by rote. Liturgical leaders need the vision to see beyond the texts on the page and decide how they may be linked to the lives of the people gathered. The texts are the primary resource for liturgical leaders, but for a liturgical celebration that is an authentic expression of the whole community's life of faith and service, more is required. Our Sunday gathering at church is the time in our lives each week when "we offer our selves, our souls and bodies." This oblation, this self-offering, is at the heart of the meaning of Christian worship, but the offering of our bodies cannot be merely theoretical. It requires *enactment*.

In the early church, we have evidence of important ritual movements involving not only the clergy and ministers, but the whole people of God. In one seventh-century document called the First Roman Ordo, we find a description of the celebration of Easter at Rome, where throughout the entire liturgy the community was in constant movement. It included three great processions, two of which involved the laity. The first procession was of the clergy and assisting ministers as they entered the building where the people had gathered, but the other two processions belonged to the people. The first procession of the people focused upon the carrying of the gifts to the altar, including not merely the bread and wine to be consecrated in the

Great Thanksgiving, but also a whole array of material gifts, such as food and clothing to be taken to those in need. These were placed around the altar, acknowledged in the eucharistic prayer, and later distributed. The other procession of the people to the altar came later in the rite, when they moved forward to receive communion as the assembly of God's faithful people. All in all this great Sunday assembly was a kind of icon of the church, a public manifestation of the people of God.

These great processional rites in the ancient classical model remind us of the important role movement can play within liturgical actions. The liturgy was not merely verbal, but involved the other senses through the fragrance of incense, through gesture and touch and sound. On the whole, the dominance of the clerical model led to the eclipse of this sensual dimension. The physical richness of the rites gave way to a preoccupation with requirements regarding matter and form in order to meet the standards of canon law for validity. This concern with validity turned in upon itself. Laws intended to set a minimal standard for *recognition* (that is, conforming to the intention of the church) came to determine customary practice.[9]

This change in liturgical understanding came at a terrible price. The rites were pinned down in rubrical details that the priest was obliged to obey, such as how many times the priest was to make the sign of the cross while reciting the eucharistic prayer and the exact moments at which he was to bow his head. The power of ritual to convey any other dimensions of meaning was reduced to the esoteric. The sense of mystery as the revelation of God's presence gave way to the sense of mystery as something too holy to be understood by the laity. Only the ordained might claim access to these deeper secrets of Christian faith.

It goes without saying that this distorted way of thinking turns the New Testament sense of mystery and of worship upside down.

~ Dance of Life or of Death?

A professional dancer once said to me, "Ballet reaches another level of meaning than merely movement." As I said earlier, we move because of our physical nature. Such movement can be merely functional, but because of its essential relation to human nature, movement can take on great symbolic importance, especially in dance. A couple dancing together on their fiftieth anniversary expresses much more than the movement of physical bodies. Dance is expressive of the deeper aspects of human life, and this is true whether we are talking about classic ballet or the powerful, ethnic folk dances that stir a people to joy in the celebration of their national identity. Dance is also universal as a language of communication. For Christians, we would claim that the liturgy is the enactment of our faith in ritual dance.

This power of dance to communicate meaning creates an imperative for the church to renew our rites so that liturgical prayer can employ the whole human person. Human beings pray most naturally not only with our minds and with words, but with our bodies. The earliest paintings we have of Christians at prayer shows them, men and women alike, with their arms outstretched as they offer thanksgiving to God. In the eastern church today, a Coptic priest still dances around the altar at the time of the eucharistic prayer. In the western tradition, these physical elements have been gradually eliminated until the priest is essentially "stationed" at the altar.

Given our long preoccupation with fixed liturgical texts and questions of canonical validity, recovering a more holistic sense of the role of the body in worship will not be easy. It will mean far more than merely including a few dance gestures or processions in our worship. For one thing, we will have to believe that our bodies are intended by God to be instruments of prayer, rather than inferior or evil. We will have to live out the implications of the Christian claim that in Christ God has embraced our full humanity, become enfleshed (which is what *incarnate* means), and that our bodies are called to be the holy instruments of God's grace and presence.

Today our physical bodies are often caught up in another type of movement, another dance. The poet W. H. Auden referred to our time as "the age of anxiety." Our bodies move, but their movements are frenetic. Everywhere we look in our society we find most people pulled in too many directions at once, never really living in the present moment. Our massive traffic jams witness to a society in which we all want to be someplace—any place!—other than where we are. If we have some brief time of repose, we waste it in becoming nostalgic for the past or worried about the future, but never living in the present. This, too, is a kind of dance, a dangerously dehumanizing one. It can become a dance of death—death to the soul.

To criticize this hyperactivity so characteristic of our world today is not to indulge in useless nostalgia or to devalue genuine technological advances that have made some aspects of our lives much easier. The question is, rather, of a priority of values. In the end we are human beings, not machines. Our system of values must be based upon the priorities that build up our humanity and deepen our personal relations with other human beings—our families and friends, but also those we meet along the way.

The Christian vision of all humanity united in the love of God is profoundly humane in its priorities. The Christian vision is an invitation to the dance, an invitation into a place in which our lives are shaped by the beauty and glory of God who invites us to become ever more fully human, since becoming fully human is what God has done for us. That is the model of the Incarnation. In one of the great medieval Christmas carols, the Incarnation is expressed as an invitation "to call my true love to my dance." We are called to engage our sisters and brothers in all the world in a cosmic dance that is the fulfillment of our human destiny. The goal of Christian worship is to offer us a foretaste of that eternal dance in God.[10]

Chapter Five

Whose Sacraments?

Celebrating the Signs of Baptismal Faith

A priest who was visiting a young man in prison learned that he had not received communion in over a year because the resident chaplain was of a different religious tradition. This was a serious matter for the prisoner because he was a committed Christian. What could be done? They were sitting together in a large room where perhaps a hundred prisoners were visiting with friends and family. There was anything but a prayerful silence and, even more to the point, the items that are usually required for a celebration of the eucharist were unavailable: no bread or wine, no plates or vessels. The priest realized that some creativity was required if he was to be able to respond to this situation, so he managed to obtain from the visitors' canteen a box of animal crackers and a glass of cranberry juice. Placing the animal crackers on a cardboard plate and the juice in a plastic cup, the two men sat back down together at a small table, the meal between them.

The priest began the ancient prayers with "The Lord be with you," and the young man responded, "And also with you." And so they began the Great

Thanksgiving, which has been proclaimed for two millennia "wherever two or three are gathered together" in the name of Christ. And they knew Christ present in their midst, and they ate and drank in memory of him as Christians have done since the Lord's resurrection.

I will come back to this story later, but I want to begin with it as a way of focusing the question posed by the title of this chapter: "Whose sacraments?" To whom do the sacraments belong? One answer that should be familiar to many Episcopalians comes from *The Book of Common Prayer*, where the "outline of the faith" defines the sacraments as "outward and visible signs of inward and spiritual grace, *given by Christ* as sure and certain means by which we receive that grace" (BCP 857, italics added). The answer, then, is clear—the sacraments belong not to the ordained nor even to the church as an institution, but to Christ, who first gave them to us.

Yet what does this mean for us as Christians? Although the whole Christian community would agree that the sacraments have their source in Christ, how individual Christians understand that claim varies greatly. Does it mean, for example, that in his earthly ministry Jesus explicitly instituted each of the actions that the church claims as sacramental? If so, are there seven or merely two—baptism and eucharist? Did Jesus authorize the exact set of words that are required for these sacramental actions to be authentic? Did he determine what the church has traditionally called "the matter of the sacrament," such as the use of bread and wine in the eucharist? If so, what kind of bread—leavened or unleavened? And what kind of wine—red or white? Does our prison eucharist of animal crackers and cranberry juice "count" as a sacrament?

In other words, the shared Christian view that the sacraments derive their authority and power from Christ, and that they are in some sense *instituted* by Christ, still leaves a range of very important questions to ask. How we answer questions like these will determine the way in which a particular sacramental action is performed. In other words, how a particular action unfolds within a community's public worship is shaped in significant ways by the manner in which that tradition interprets its own fidelity to Christ as the source of these actions. In our prison eucharist, fidelity to Christ is much more than using the authorized form and matter for the eucharistic rite. "Fidelity" presses us down into a deeper level of meaning, where we ask what the sign of eucharistic sharing has meant and continues to mean in the sacramental lives of Christians of every generation. The externals used in the performance of this table ritual have varied enormously over the centuries, but they have, as an act of faith by those gathered, been faithful to the meaning of the Last Supper as given to the church in the gospels. At all times and in all places the church has "done this" in memory of Christ. In the words of the great Anglican scholar Dom Gregory Dix, "week by week and month by month, on a hundred thousand successive Sundays, faithfully, unfailingly, across all the parishes of christendom, the pastors have done this just to *make* the *plebs sancta Dei*—the holy common people of God."[1]

Moreover, it is terribly important to recognize how significant our responses to such questions are as we move forward into the twenty-first century and away from an ethos that was dominated for so many centuries by the customs and constraints of medieval society. We have considered these cultural forms in previous chapters, such as the fixed shape of the liturgy under the control of a clerical hierarchy. Once they became the norm, these liturgical customs continued to shape the church's expectations regarding sacramental worship even as the secular world moved into the modern era of increasing cultural pluralism. A particularly significant turning point in this regard was the ninth century, which marked a retrenchment on the part of the church as the various national cultures of Europe began to take shape.[2] This development, growing out of the imposed cultural unity of western Catholic Christendom, brought the challenge of cultural diversity into a situation where the imperial need for political unity reinforced the church's adherence to the Latin liturgical tradition.

Such a transition holds far-reaching implications for the liturgy in its adaptation to a multicultural world, and some of these implications have to do with *meaning*. What does it *mean* to adapt the sacramental rites of the church in this way? Do we not risk a change in their meaning? Which aspects of a sacrament may change? Which are immutable? How can we tell the difference? Can the "outward and visible signs" be altered and yet remain the appointed means of "inward and spiritual grace"?[3]

～ A Common Recognition

One aspect of these questions about the sacraments is ecclesial, for we are talking about fundamental actions that reveal the faith of the gathered community that celebrates them. Our understanding of the sacraments should not be abstract or merely theoretical—sacraments are always known in the *doing* of them. Sacraments are distinctive to a gathering of Christians who live at a specific time and place within a particular culture. For this reason, the significance of what I call "shared recognition" is crucial. Do the people who are gathered together *recognize* this sacramental action as revealing Christ's presence in their lives?

My reason for emphasizing "recognition" is that the sacraments have been traditionally understood as a building up of the unity of the body of Christ. The sacrament of Holy Baptism, for example, actually *creates* the unity of that body, while the eucharist—as we hear echoed in the familiar phrase, "one bread, one body"—is the sign of our unity in Christ. So wherever this gathering takes place, whether it is in Berkeley or New York, Calcutta or Rome, or in a small village church, everyone who takes part must be able to "recognize" that this sacramental action is what the church claims it to be. Doubt, or a failure to recognize, would reveal a division within the assembly that erodes the essential purpose of the sacraments to reveal the church's unity.[4]

This raises the issue of *validity* in its relationship to meaning. "Validity" is sometimes misunderstood as the high point of sacramental meaning, but it is far from that. It is a term related to canon law, which sets the minimal standards by which a sacramental act is recognized as authentic by the church. On the whole, preoccupation with validity has been a marked characteristic of the clerical mindset. In the Middle Ages, especially during times of very low standards in the education of rural clergy, the bishops were concerned that significant parts of the eucharistic rite might be eliminated by a priest who was poorly educated or could barely read. This situation quite understandably led to the fixation not only of rites but also of ritual norms (such as signs of the cross and other gestures) so that a person preparing for ordination, no matter how minimal his education, would learn a fixed routine to guarantee that the minimal requirements for the eucharist were being met.

When I speak of "recognition," on the other hand, I am deliberately placing the question of the authenticity of the eucharist into a larger and more ecclesial framework. Does this meal shared by a group of believing Christians adhere to the meaning of its institution by Jesus among his followers? Here the question is clearly in the context of faith, rather than rubrics. I was privileged to participate in such a eucharist in the mid-1960s in Denmark, when I was invited to be present at a private gathering of Danish Roman Catholics and Protestants for a shared celebration of the eucharist—which their respective traditions would not have seen as legitimate. The ritual pattern was very simple; we did not use the official rite of any tradition. Rather, we reflected together on the word of God in the readings, and then we offered thanksgiving to God over the bread and wine in spontaneous prayer, and then shared the holy gifts. Was this the eucharist? With regard to official authorization, no, it was not. Was it the eucharist for this gathering of Christ's followers? Yes, beyond the shadow of a doubt. This is what I mean when I say that "recognition" pushes us to a deeper level of engagement with the signs of the church's fundamental unity.[5]

Another example will help us see the importance of the dimension beyond mere validity. Let us consider the ordination of a group of women to the priesthood of the Episcopal Church ("the Philadelphia Eleven"), which took place in 1974. The response within the Episcopal Church to this action immediately brought this key question of recognition to the fore. Many supporters of the ordination of women immediately recognized this rite as a prophetic act and the women themselves as priests of the church, speaking of them as "irregular but valid." This meant that the women were indeed priests, but that the performance of their ministries had not been authorized by the church. Others did not extend this recognition, for a variety of reasons believing that these women had not been ordained as priests. Some insisted that women by nature simply cannot be ordained: only males, they said, are the proper "matter" of this sacrament. (Here we see the influence of the canonical mindset that is concerned to define in detail and usually in exclusive terms the required "matter" for a sacrament.) Even John Coburn, later Bishop of Massachusetts and a staunch supporter of the ordination of women, and at that time president of the House of Deputies of the General Convention, held that the Episcopal Church did not have ordained women priests. His point was that there was no official consensus upon which to base the authorization of the ordination. Without that canonical foundation, there was a fundamental lack of consensus with regard to what I have called "recognition."

In other words, for some Episcopalians the women were indeed priests; for others, they were not. With the General Convention of 1976 the needed canonical changes were voted to establish an adequate consensus on this question. This may seem to be a legalistic approach, and yet the canons of the church do serve the important function of establishing a common ground for recognition. The canons indicate the consensus at which the church's members have arrived— at least for one particular time and context, since canon law is sometimes changed when the church moves into a new situation. But without the common ground that the canons supply, individuals or groups may *believe* their actions to be justified, but of course the goal of unity is shattered.

There are still laity and clergy in the Episcopal Church who do not recognize the ordination of women to the episcopate and the presbyterate. Differences of opinion on lesser matters do not seriously affect the unity of the church, but on major issues such as women's ordination the church must rely on its canonical norms to establish the perimeters of recognition. This is the point that John Coburn was making, and it is an essential one in the life of the church today, as we engage a wide range of serious issues that undermine Christ's imperative to us "that they may all be one." Schism is the easy choice for those who refuse to engage others in finding the common ground, and so Christian unity becomes further eroded.

∼ Sacraments and Cultural Symbols

Adapting the sacraments to widely diverse cultures raises profound questions that go beyond the various options the rubrics offer in *The Book of Common Prayer.* Yet far too often even these options are ignored and a fixed pattern of prayers and ritual actions becomes standardized. Often, for example, virtually no ritual distinction is made between the principal celebration of the eucharist on a Sunday and a simple weekday celebration, at least with regard to the texts. Frequently the rubrics indicate that a text "may" be said—such as the phrases known as the Comfortable Words that are printed after the absolution (BCP 332), but are not required. In the same way, the prayer immediately before communion known as the Prayer of Humble Access (BCP 337) is optional, but many Anglicans are so accustomed to it that they are seriously disturbed if it is omitted. Hence such options are often ignored, even when the specific context of a eucharist would warrant them. At an early weekday celebration of the eucharist that people might attend on their way to work, for example, there is no inherent reason why the service should not be simplified for the sake of time. Yet often all the same texts are included that would be part of the full Sunday celebration of the eucharist. This is indicative of how strong the tendency is toward rigid liturgical models that insists the rites unfold always in precisely the same way.

Diversity even within a single parish's liturgical practice is often difficult to achieve. Both clergy and laity feel at home in a fixed pattern, so that any change is looked upon as disruptive. It is important to take this into account when we start to think about more far-reaching changes that may be required if our rites are to incarnate radically different cultures and places. The extreme liturgical stability that we all have become accustomed to over the centuries does create a hostile environment for change—even changes that bring new life and are faithful to the underlying intention of the sacramental signs.

As I pointed out earlier in the chapter on culture, Anglicans have almost grudgingly acknowledged the imperatives posed by the planting of Christian faith in non-Anglo cultures, even in the important area of language. But authentic adaptation does not mean that we simply modify classical Anglican rites for a culture that is quite alien to them; rather, what is required is inculturation. When some fundamental aspect of the church's life and teaching—such as one of the sacraments—takes a very different cultural form, inculturation has occurred. Thus it is singularly important that the church have clarity concerning the meaning behind the sacraments as it explores new cultural expressions of these acts that have traditionally had a central role in the life of the church.

For a symbol to be effective, what it signifies must be evident, recognizable to the people of that culture. This offers us a clue as to why the religious traditions of American origin generally consider themselves to be non-sacramental. The churches with a strong sacramental foundation are, without exception, grounded in their origins in western medieval culture. In other words, the symbolic actions of Roman Catholics, Lutherans, and Episcopalians are based upon "imported" modes of symbolization that were integral to the religious faith and practice of the early settlers and missionaries of those traditions.

Religious pluralism characterized the American colonies prior to the Revolution. Once we had become an independent nation, the young United States established a constitutional separation of church and state, a separation that had not been characteristic in the nations of origin from which the settlers had come. Often it was the *oppression* of church and state establishments (such as that found in England and the German states) that many of the early settlers were seeking to escape. In such a context, it was perhaps inevitable that the European-born liturgical traditions (and here I am thinking particularly of Anglicans, Lutherans, and Roman Catholics) would be inclined *not* to adapt their sacramental practices to the new culture since, in the pluralistic society in which they found themselves, their religious practice was an essential dimension of their identity and unity.

So these religious traditions continued to use the sacramental forms they had known in Europe, with only minimal modification. Groups of non-English-speaking origin often preserved the language of their home culture for at least one generation and sometimes longer; Episcopalians, in effect, did the same thing by preserving the use of an increasingly archaic liturgical English. Because of the importance of a defined religious identity, moreover, these models continued to shape the sacramental understanding and expectations of later generations, often even continuing to use their original languages. When someone decided, perhaps through marriage, to enter one of these traditions—either from another denomination or from a non-religious background—this often meant taking on to some degree the cultural ethos of the nation from which that religious community had emerged. I have observed this particularly among friends who have entered the Greek Orthodox tradition for theological reasons or through marriage. In due course, these friends have commented to me that their difficulties did not lie in the area of doctrine or even with the liturgical practice of the tradition adopted, but rather with the strong ethnic ethos of the tradition to which they remained, at least to some degree, always an outsider.

Such adherence to the culture of the society of origin, however, has not always been characteristic of the Christian tradition. When we consider the New Testament, for example, a stunning example of cultural inclusivity is immediately available to us. During the period of the earliest Christian communities, the shift from a predominantly Jewish context into the Gentile society was fraught with difficulties. The Book of Acts records that Paul and Barnabas were appointed to go to the church at Jerusalem and consult with the apostles and elders on the question of Gentile circumcision (Acts 15:2). Should the Gentile converts be required to obey the Jewish cultic practices that Jesus and the apostles took for granted? It was the testimony of Peter that carried the day: "Why are you putting God to the test by placing on the neck of the disciples a yoke that neither our ancestors nor we have been able to bear? On the contrary, we believe that we will be saved through the grace of the Lord Jesus, just as they will" (15:10-11). Therefore this requirement was not imposed upon the Gentile converts and so a significant page was turned in universalizing the Christian proclamation.

We can see a liturgical example of this flexibility with regard to other cultural elements in the situation in the ninth century, when the Emperor Charlemagne authorized the copying of the liturgical books of the city of Rome for diffusion in his northern European kingdom. The emperor apparently saw a certain liturgical unity as a reinforcement of the unity that he sought for his empire. Yet when these books were copied for use in the north, a kind of supplement was added with materials that were already established in the liturgical practice in the north. Thus the local customs, including a great deal of ceremonial as well as commemorations of saints unknown in Rome, were incorporated into the newly imposed Roman rite. This eventually led to the fusion of these elements into the then emerging altar missal to be used by the priest at mass. In this we see the creation of a whole new model of liturgy for the western church.[6]

In the early centuries of Christianity, the unity of the church did not require conformity to a single liturgical norm. By the eleventh century, however, an increasing demand for ritual conformity arose out of a desire for political conformity and obedience. Furthermore, the invention of printing in the fifteenth century greatly increased the church's ability to require conformity by controlling the flow and uniformity of printed matter, a significant factor in both the reformed and counter-reformed traditions.

In spite of this narrowing of the liturgical tradition to a set of specified liturgical texts, Christian history also offers us a more inclusive model. The Christian faith has always been embodied in some cultural form; in fact, it does not exist apart from that. This means that even a trans-cultural model—one that claims to be universal, detached from any particular culture—is always shaped by the manners and customs of the culture in which it originated. The fact that secular culture has continued to develop while the sacred culture has remained fixed does not change the fact of cultural specificity in its origins. In the major liturgical traditions, however, the hallowed status of these unchanging sacred models allowed them to remain viable expressions of religious faith in a society in which the realms of sacred and secular remained distinct.

∾ Sacraments and Community

I have argued throughout this book that religion is not merely a matter of personal choice, but an integral aspect of one's relation to the world. Nor are the sacraments private actions on the part of individuals, no matter how much we may try to interpret them as acts of private piety and thus optional to the Christian life. Sacramental actions always pertain to the corporate life of the whole Christian community and their purpose is to build up its unity in a common life and faith. This is why I emphasize so strongly the importance of a shared *recognition* of what these actions mean within a Christian community. That meaning is never a private or individual matter.

Yet if the sacraments are always embodied within some specific cultural forms, and if the church of our time has entered upon a multicultural era more diverse than at any other time in history, how are we to resolve questions that are of such fundamental importance to the church's identity? How can we distinguish which aspects of a sacramental action are subject to adaptation and change? Perhaps the most immediate example that comes to mind is the one seen in the story that begins this chapter—that is, the question of the "matter" of the eucharist, the bread and wine. We see in these elements two levels of meaning. At the natural level they are symbols of human nourishment, and as such—as ordinary food of the table—Jesus took them and associated them with his self-offering to God. At the same time, bread and wine are also historical symbols, the same *kind* of food and drink taken by Jesus at the last meal with his followers. At which level do they operate for us—as natural symbols or as historical symbols? We must, I think, respond that they operate at both levels.

In liturgical practice, we have for centuries emphasized the *historical* level—namely, that it was with bread and wine that Jesus instituted the eucharist. In recent years much liturgical renewal has been concerned to remind us that this sacred meal is still a *meal*. Although our bread and wine is not exactly like the bread and wine Jesus and his disciples ate and drank that last night, they do correspond more or less. But what about the *natural* level of the symbol? What if we found ourselves in a situation in which bread and wine were unobtainable, as has sometimes been true during wartime? Or, given our concern here with issues of cultural relevance, what if bread and wine as we know them in our culture were unknown or at least alien to another culture in which Christians wish to gather to celebrate the eucharist? Can other elements that correspond in meaning to the basic food and drink that bread and wine represented in Jewish culture be used? The multicultural world in which we are living requires us to look more openly at such questions.

Not too many years ago, it was not unusual for the entire circle of one's family and friends to be members of one religious tradition. I have friends who speak to me of a childhood in which everyone they knew was a part of the same religious tradition. That this was true in Europe is not surprising, since large national areas were often strongly identified with one religion, but religious homogeneity was also true in regions of the United States as well. I once had an Irish Roman Catholic friend tell me that when he grew up in Philadelphia, their neighborhood was entirely Irish or Italian Roman Catholic, and that he did not know anyone even of another Christian tradition until he went to college. We are not living in such a world today: now we coexist with other world religions at virtually all levels of our daily lives.

In addition to this type of religious diversity, all people of faith find themselves living in a secular society that claims indifference to religious (as opposed to spiritual) concerns. To Christians formed in the transcultural model, this break within the social fabric may not seem strange; American culture has inclined all of us toward a view of religion as essentially an individual affair. Ironically, it is the militant Christian right with its strong individualistic overtones that is often able to insert its views into the national debates, since the sacramental traditions have been generally ineffective in shaping a coherent public position that can offer another "religious" option to American society.

In such a complex and charged situation, does the church dare to consider a radical adaptation of the sacraments—the sacred actions that are so profoundly linked to Christian identity and faith? In spite of the complexity, the cultural pluralism of our world really leaves us with no response other than yes. The Christian faith is rooted in the theology of the

Incarnation, the claim that in Jesus of Nazareth, the eternal God has "tabernacled" among us. God has made a home in the human community, not only as its source and creator, but also as the One who has shared our life and has thus embraced the whole human family. To make this claim, religious faith must take the created world very seriously indeed and value its every dimension. The diversity of cultures is thus not a hindrance to Christian faith, but rather an expression of God's wonderful creativity.

～ What Makes a Sacrament "Christian"?

In such a view of creation, it is inevitable that fundamental aspects of the human experience will enjoy similar religious meanings even in diverse religious and cultural contexts. For example, the water that Christians associate with the rite of baptism, with its capacity to cleanse and refresh us, is a common element shared by all human beings. This capacity is not something that needs to be explained: our bodies "know" the power of water to cleanse and renew without using words to define it. Similarly, our bodies "know" that bread and wine, food and drink, nourish and sustain us. In the depth of its being, an infant knows that it must eat and drink in order to live. This knowledge does not depend upon verbal instruction; it is written into our bodies.

So when we turn to consider the sacraments of Christian baptism and eucharist, we see that they are based upon universal experiences shared by all human beings. Their religious significance is based upon their correspondence to our physical humanity. And since washing and the taking of food and drink are common to all humanity, it is also inevitable that in other societies, including primitive communities, these actions likewise tend toward religious significance.

Anthropologists have found that virtually all societies perform rites of washing that fulfill a symbolic representation of cleansing and incorporation into membership of the community. Similarly, we find ritual meals that are expressive of the common life of a community. Obviously there are significant differences of meaning and context between one community and another, but these acts are still sacramental in nature because they are outward signs of another level of meaning.

What, then, makes these ritual actions of washing and of eating a common meal specifically Christian? What makes a symbol "Christian"? If the making of symbols is a shared human activity, working with the same basic materials of human life, how does the meaning of these acts find an integral place in the context of Christian faith?

Scripture

Can the Bible establish what is specifically Christian? The faith-symbols that emerge from the Bible belong to particular cultures, times, and places that are not our own. So from the very beginning we are involved in adapting these symbols to our own time. Christian baptism, for example, has undergone adaptation from the very beginning. In the gospels we have the witness of the baptism of Jesus in the Jordan River, and yet in Christian practice throughout two millennia, this water rite of incorporation into the community of the church has been endlessly adapted. A second-century document known as *The Didache* describes how baptism is to be performed: cold running water, like the stream of a river (as in the baptism of Jesus), is the preferred method. But the document goes on to say, "If you do not have running water, baptize in some other. If you cannot in cold, then in warm. If you have neither, then pour water on the head three times 'in the name of the Father, Son, and Holy Spirit'"[7] What we see here, in the period immediately after the time of the apostles, is a genuine openness to adaptation. This adaptation has been characteristic of every successive culture throughout history in which the Christian proclamation has taken place. So although the Bible remains the privileged expression of the Judeo-Christian story of God's relation to the created world, what is called "the history of salvation," it cannot be claimed as the normative guide to Christian worship. The worship of the Christian community has always adapted to the realities of how people live, and that continues to be true for the church today.

However, the Bible does establish the frame of reference for Christian identity, and so we must ask if biblical symbols such as circumcision and Passover, or baptism and the eucharist, define the absolute norm for Christian symbolization. Yet as soon as we ask the question in this way, we recognize that in practice we have already been selective. For example, Christians have not maintained the symbolic rituals required by the Hebrew scriptures, as we saw in the debate over circumcision recorded in Acts 15. Adaptation is, in fact, the rule. But if this is so, by what criteria are we to determine what must *not* change?

This question evokes the memory of the debate that began in the sixteenth century in the English church as to the authority of the Bible in matters related to public worship. The Puritan party took an extreme Calvinist line on this issue, insisting that the Bible was the absolute authority for the establishment of liturgical practices. Any custom that was not authorized in the Bible was "an invention of men," and so must be rejected. Yet even in Calvin's own church in Geneva so strict a line could not be enforced, and other rites were admitted so long as they were not seen to conflict with scripture. The Puritan objections to these "inventions of men," which they found everywhere in the 1559 *Book of Common Prayer* during the reign of Queen Elizabeth I, eventually led them into separation from the established church and in due course to America. Yet clearly our celebration of sacramental rites always involves us with such "inventions"—they are, in fact, the instrumental means through which the culture of the gathered community is expressed. Just as the sacramental rites found in the Bible are rooted in the faith-experience of their societies of origin, so the celebration of those actions in other contexts has involved Christians in adapting them to other cultures and to new situations. The church's life does not unfold in a static environment, and the Bible alone cannot give to the church in any age a complete model for such rites, nor on its own establish what is specifically Christian.

Instituted by Jesus

We also have what is generally called the criterion of "dominical institution," or what has been "established by the Lord." This phrase refers to the view that the church's sacramental actions are those that Jesus himself instituted during his ministry. One of the important divisive issues at the time of the Reformation in the sixteenth century concerned the *number* of sacraments that Jesus explicitly instituted, but on both sides of the argument it was agreed that such institution was required for these acts to be an authentic part of the Christian tradition. The Roman Church argued for seven sacraments, a pattern that had been systematized in the twelfth century and from that time had enjoyed the general consensus of the western church. The reformers, on the other hand, insisted that Jesus' institution of the sacrament must be *explicit*, not merely implied, and hence only the sacraments of baptism and eucharist could be accepted.

The problem with this debate for us today is that such a naive and literal use of the scriptural texts inhibits our understanding of the biblical material in its original context. When we look, for example, at the Great Commission in the gospel of Matthew, where Jesus commands the apostles to "go therefore and make disciples of all nations, baptizing them in the name of the Father and of the Son and of the Holy Spirit" (28:19), we in fact have an image of the practice of baptism in the life of Matthew's community at about the end of the first century. In other words, this passage in the gospel of Matthew establishes the church's practice of baptism upon the authority of Jesus, but it is as that authority was being expressed within the ongoing life of the community.

Hence, the "trinitarian formula" attributed to Jesus is in fact a theological formulation that developed several decades after the resurrection of Jesus. Although these words could not have been the actual words of Jesus, they do indicate that for the community in which Matthew lived, the practice of baptism rested clearly upon an implicit authorization coming from Christ. This is where we see the framework for the debate about dominical institution: Does such institution mean that Jesus *literally* spoke certain words (as if we had a recording) or that a certain practice was instituted by the church in the years following the resurrection as it sought to live out his message? Fundamentalists would say that if we do not have the literal words, we have nothing. Those of us who see the church as the place in which we engage the living Lord would say that we have everything.[8]

What we *do* have in the passage from Matthew is an important *witness* to the practice of baptism as rooted in the life and authority of Jesus, giving us insight into this practice as it was developing in the early Christian community at the time Matthew wrote. In other words, we find in Matthew an already emerging sense of tradition with regard to the sacrament of baptism in Christianity. Rather than requiring explicit authorization by Jesus, we see this early community shaping its corporate life within the society of faith that emerged in the wake of Christ's death and resurrection. The institution, I would suggest, was grounded in their own identity as the body of Christ. We shall return to this point shortly, but first let us consider an often-invoked third criterion for determining what may be accepted as authentic Christian practice.

Tradition
Since the strength of the authority of tradition is based on how far back the tradition goes and how long it has been shaping a given practice, it is a criterion of considerable importance among the liturgical churches. Tradition commands a natural respect because its authority is grounded in an experience of the church that has extended over many generations and even over national boundaries. Perhaps the most powerful example of the force of tradition is seen in the long-standing stability of certain elements of the eucharist in the Roman Catholic Church prior to the Second Vatican Council. A significant part of the eucharistic prayer, although not all of it, dates back to the fourth century, and many other prayers of the rite are of comparable antiquity. The stability of this tradition had preserved it, and even reinforced it at the time of the Reformation.

For Anglicans, a similar authority has developed with regard to the texts that were prepared by Archbishop Thomas Cranmer. As with the prayers of the Roman rite, the two prayer books prepared by Cranmer in 1549 and 1552 have been the source of a long, evolving tradition among the provinces of the Anglican Communion. For Anglicans they have served as the defining resource for later liturgical developments.

The liturgical reforms of Archbishop Cranmer were quite radical, for reasons both theological and cultural. The use of the vernacular was, of course, an imperative that emerged from the culture: Latin was no longer a language understood by most of the people. But new theological imperatives also required a reshaping of traditional texts as well as the crafting of new ones, texts that would be more accountable to a theology that was faithful to scripture. A good example of this theological transformation is seen in Cranmer's translations of the traditional Latin collects, specifically those for the feast days of saints. In the medieval tradition, these prayers often invoked the prayers of the particular saint. This view of the relation of the saints to the church on earth was generally rejected by the reformers, who saw no need for any intermediary between God and humankind than Christ himself, "our only Mediator and Advocate."[9] Yet because of the importance of the Latin rite in the religious life of the English people, and their shared sense that Latin was a sacred language essential to sacred actions, the reforms of Cranmer met with opposition and even, during the brief reign of Queen Mary, with complete rejection. It is thus all the more ironic that once they were reauthorized during the reign of Elizabeth I, the Cranmerian texts gradually achieved acceptance as the language of worship in England, and thus became the standard for later versions of the rites not only within the Anglican Communion but in other Christian traditions as well. Some of Cranmer's texts, for example, found their way into the Methodist rites of the Wesleys, as one might expect, but also into English translations in the United States when Lutheran rites needed to be adapted to the American vernacular. This gave to Cranmer's texts, even beyond the Anglican Communion, a kind of priority status for liturgical rites in English. Thus Cranmer's liturgical English became as resistant to change as the Latin rites of the sixteenth century.

This opposition to change is exactly the problem in allowing tradition to be an absolute criterion for determining which sacramental rites and practices are most adequate to the expression of their Christian content. When a tradition has used a fixed set of authorized liturgical rites over a long period of time, those forms enter deeply into the religious conscious-ness of the people. One example is the significant role the Prayer of Humble Access (BCP 337) has played in Anglican eucharistic piety. The prayer is, of course, devotional; it does not fulfill any essential role within the eucharistic action, so in recent decades liturgical reformers have believed its use should at least be optional, and removed in more contemporary rites. But the text is also one of exceptional beauty whose place just prior to communion intensified its devo-tional importance for Anglicans through centuries of use. This was brought home to me when a new stu-dent at Nashotah House asked me with considerable emotion, "Why have you removed the Prayer of Humble Access from Rite II?" I replied, "We have not removed it; it was never there." It took a while for her to see my point since in her home parish, because the people loved the prayer, it had been kept in celebrations of Rite II so that, the rector hoped, the introduction of Rite II might go more smoothly. For many people, their whole religious experience and the nurturing of their faith seem to be essentially linked to those familiar forms that they have heard and said over the years.

✦ Sacraments and Renewal

Yet tradition is not always a reactionary or conservative force. When we look at tradition in its full scope and recognize the historical developments that have come together to form it, we may also find the sources for radical renewal. Tradition is not merely the practices of the recent past—even though the liturgical memory of each generation is limited to its own experience. That is why history is the great liberator; it offers us the knowledge that things have not been always as they were in the recent past. For example, in the twentieth century, especially due to the wide ecumenical influence of Vatican Council II, both Anglicans and Roman Catholics saw the conservative force of tradition vigorously confronted by new priorities—the recovery of a baptismal ecclesiology and the renewal of the church's worship in a multicultural world. In some fundamental ways, World War II served as a catalyst on some of these questions, when Christians of different traditions found themselves imprisoned together under the Nazi tyranny. Denominational differences and barriers faded in significance when compared to the fundamental unity of their common faith in Jesus Christ.

Yet this unity of baptismal faith was also being recognized within an increasingly complex and diverse world culture, and Christians began to explore liturgical and sacramental models that seemed more appropriate to their particular life and culture. How can we determine today which models and practices reflect adaptations that do not distort or lose sight of Christian identity? I would like to offer a response to this question that brings together the three criteria that we have already considered—biblical authority, institution by Jesus, and tradition—but unites them in a new perspective.

The early Christian communities that we see mirrored in the gospels and the epistles of the New Testament show a full range of local adaptations to their common identity as the body of Christ. To choose but one example of this, we might note the extraordinary diversity of ministerial models found in the New Testament writings. Although as Anglicans we have always affirmed the threefold pattern of bishop, priest, and deacon that emerged as normative in the second century, the first century of Christianity saw a great deal of local variation with regard to the church's leadership. Some of these roles we can recognize as "designated," that is, authorized through prayer and the laying on of hands. With others, we simply see people fulfilling needed ministries within the various communities. Even the roles of "overseer" (*episcopos*) and elder (*presbuteros*) are not consistently distinguished in the New Testament. We should be cautious about reading backward into these writings developments from a later period.

Thus the witness of scripture does not, as Calvin suggested, supply for the church an absolute model for Christian liturgical practice. In other words, the New Testament does not offer a pattern for Christian community and its worship to which every succeeding generation must conform. Rather, the Christian scriptures express what was distinctive in the lives of each of these communities as they struggled to realize themselves as part of the body of Christ. Yet these communities, we assume, adapted to their particular cultures and local customs without losing their Christian identity.

As the sacramental life of the church began to take shape, we can see the primary role of the Bible in regard to Christian worship. It is the necessary reference point. The New Testament offers a witness to Christ Jesus to which all later generations that would call themselves Christian must be accountable. Yet that accountability is not based upon a rigid reenactment of some authorized text, but upon responding with faith to the realities of that community's life in the world. Belief in the Incarnation means that the mystery of God's redeeming love revealed in Jesus may take flesh, may take physical expression, in every culture on earth. The question for us is always, "How can we, assembled here in the name of Christ, best celebrate the signs of our shared baptismal faith? How can we be most faithful in our response to the love of God that is revealed in Jesus?" Every assembly of the church today, in every place, is being challenged to answer that question for themselves in a rapidly changing world. Such an approach does not mean that we have to throw away our theological inheritance from past generations of Christianity. It *is* imperative for each age and culture to add its voice so that the tradition is perpetually renewed and enriched.

What, then, of the authority we ascribe to the words of Jesus? Generally when writers refer to the institution of the sacraments by Jesus, they are speaking specifically of words he said during his lifetime that are witnessed to by the New Testament. For example, the gospels of Matthew, Mark, and Luke all record Jesus' words at his final meal with his disciples, and these words are seen to authorize the sacrament of the eucharist. But perhaps this understanding is too limited an approach to how Christ continues to work in the life of the church today and into the future. Is it possible to think of "established by Christ" in another way—as a process of dynamic unfolding within the church? Can we understand it not as events restricted to the experiences of the first disciples, but rather as continuing actions of Christ present and active within the community of his followers today?

These actions may have been first instituted during the ministry of Jesus and his apostles, but they have also developed through history as the church continually finds itself in changing cultures and with changing pastoral needs. Such changes may be found in abundance in the modifications in practice and even of meaning in the evolution of the sacramental rites through history. One example is the Great Thanksgiving of the eucharistic rite. This central prayer of the eucharistic assembly has taken a wide variety of forms over history. Some early versions were very brief;[10] later, under the influence of increasing clerical power, the prayer became much longer as it subsumed other dimensions of the rite into its framework, including the Prayers of the People. The shift of the intercessory prayers into the eucharistic prayer is a powerful example of the eclipse of lay participation in the liturgy. Given this well-documented evolution in virtually every aspect of the liturgical rites, we cannot hold rigidly to the precise forms developed in the past, whether first-century Palestine or twelfth-century Europe. To fail to address this challenge would indicate an unwillingness to trust in the continuing guidance of the Holy Spirit.

As we learn to be more flexible in interpreting the criteria of scripture, dominical institution, and tradition, we must not lose sight of their fundamental significance. Obviously, adaptation cannot contradict the plain sense of scripture: the water rite of baptism could not be replaced by walking the labyrinth! Nor could the sacred meal of the faith community be replaced by some action unrelated to human nourishment, such as the giving of alms or washing of feet. As we have seen earlier, the sacramental sense of these fundamental Christian rites is grounded in the basic human actions of bathing and eating in the context of a community. That is the ground level of their meaning.

Likewise, any adaptation needs to express continuity with the tradition as a living dimension of the Christian life. This means that tradition is not merely the restraining hand of the past on the life of the church today, but rather an ever-renewed treasury of the church's life. It should remind us perpetually that the church never exists as some ideal vision of the past—the apostolic period, the high Middle Ages, or the Reformation. There is no ideal time in the church's history that should determine norms of Christian life and worship in radically different times and places. When a Christian community gathers for the eucharist, the whole of the tradition is carried by that community: we are members of a vast human society that has assembled in every time and place on earth to perform the awesome and simple action of eating and drinking together in the name of Jesus Christ.

◈ Whose Sacraments?

To whom do the sacraments belong? They belong to Christ. We return to our original answer. To say that the sacraments are Christ's implies that they have been "instituted" from within the body of his followers: they are instituted by the body of Christ and thus display as they evolve through time the changing contexts in which Christians have gathered in worship, professing their faith and offering themselves to God. That fundamental act of Christian identity—gathering in the name of Christ—can take place not only in church buildings and homes, but even in unlikely times and places. This basic "energy" that faith draws on to express itself in sacramental signs can break in upon us as an imperative that is indifferent to the details of ritual. That is why I began this chapter with the story of an improvised eucharistic meal in a prison visiting room, using the only elements available—animal crackers on a cardboard plate and cranberry juice in a plastic cup. Was that action faithful to the institution of Christ? Did it conform to the model of scripture? Did it fulfill the expectations of the tradition? Can we give any answer other than an emphatic "yes!"?

Does this mean that the texts and rites of our liturgical tradition should be cast aside as excess baggage? If we say "no" to that question, as I feel we must, then we are obliged to add "but at the same time. . . . " No, the inherited tradition, our rites and music and vesture, should not be cast aside: they express the continuity of the church's liturgical life. But at the same time we have to remember that Christian people can be seduced into giving too high a priority to rites and the various familiar externals of public worship, while not paying attention to what the rites are intended to signify.

The eucharist celebrated in the prison is a vivid reminder of what the eucharist is about at its center of meaning: our continual remembrance of the presence of Christ in the lives of believers. In this we are not passive onlookers in a precisely defined, carefully orchestrated ritual. Rather we are called to embody the meaning of the remembrance of Christ in terms of our reality: in other words, our gathering for the eucharist is the intense focus and reminder of the presence of the risen Christ with, in, and among the people of God. But this awesome significance must not lead us to turn inward and cultivate these liturgical acts as a sacred domain quite apart from our daily lives. The eucharistic rite always sends us forth "into the world, rejoicing in the power of the Spirit." Just as the Incarnation is a principle of God's participation in human life embodied in Jesus, so the institution of the sacraments is an extension of the ministry of Jesus through his Body throughout every generation. We must take very seriously the claim that Christ continues to be present in the life of the church. This presence is God's gift and does not depend upon a particular set of external rites or places or vesture. What God does require on our part is faith.

In each celebration of the eucharist, the words of the Great Thanksgiving lead us to join our voices with those of the heavenly choir in the ancient hymn of praise and glory to our God. We sing, "Holy, holy, holy Lord, God of power and might, heaven and earth are full of your glory." It is easy for us to imagine that *heaven* is filled with the glory of God because it is still beyond our experience. But it is more difficult for us to believe that the *earth* is likewise filled with the glory of God. We know the earth all too well, and it is often a place of pain and human destitution, of war and destruction, of waste and futility.

How can we claim that the earth is filled with the glory of God? That is precisely where sacrament is essential for the life of faith. We humans are "of the earth," but it is that earth, the dust to which we shall return, that God has embraced and fulfilled in the Incarnation of Jesus Christ. In the light of the Incarnation, the whole created, physical world has the capacity to become the place in which God dwells, in every part and in each one of us. Our human, physical dust has been transformed and fulfilled by grace, and so each human being, created in the image of God, has the inherent capacity to be *in our physical nature* a revelation of the divine presence. As the people of God, we are the witnesses to that grace by which all created things are sustained in being. Our dust, our humanity, is shot through with hints of glory. And that dust finds its deepest fulfillment in the praise of God.

Endnotes

Chapter 1: Which Theology?

1. The document known as *Apostolic Tradition*, attributed to the Roman presbyter Hippolytus and dated at approximately 215 C.E., offers us an array of early liturgical models that suggest a complementarity of roles between the liturgical leaders and the assembled people. See *Hippolytus: A Text for Students*, ed. G. J. Cuming, Grove Liturgical Study No. 8 (Nottingham: Grove Books, 1976).

2. Again, we have witness of this in *Apostolic Tradition*, par. 16; Cuming, *Hippolytus*, 15-16.

3. A presentation of the arguments in support of the more flexible model can be found in "Patterning the Sacraments After Christ," by Richard Fabian, in *Open* (Journal of the Associated Parishes for Liturgy and Mission), 40:3 (Fall 1994): 1-4. A brief summary of the traditional view appears in the same issue: "Should the Unbaptized Be Welcomed to the Lord's Table?" by L. L. Mitchell, pp. 5-6.

4. See Ormonde Plater, *Intercession: A Theological and Practical Guide* (Cambridge, Mass.: Cowley Publications, 1995).

∾ Chapter 2: Who Celebrates?

1. Justin Martyr, *First Apology*, chp. 65. See W. Rordorf and others, *The Eucharist of the Early Christians* (New York: Pueblo Publishing Company, 1978), 71-72. See also a discussion of the role of the presider in: R. C. D. Jasper & G. J. Cuming, *Prayers of the Eucharist: Early and Reformed* (New York: Pueblo Publishing Company, 1975), 25-26.

2. *Sacrosanctum Concilium* (4 December 1963), par. 41. Although this document was directed primarily toward liturgical reform in the Roman Catholic Church, it has during the intervening decades exerted considerable influence within all of the liturgical traditions with regard to basic principles of liturgical renewal.

3. Augustine of Hippo, Sermon 272 (dated 405-411 C.E.). *Patrologia Latina* 38.1246-1248. See D. J. Sheerin, *The Eucharist* (Wilmington, Del.: Michael Glazier, 1986), 94-96.

4. Peter Hammond, *Liturgy and Architecture* (London: Barrie and Rocklitt, 1960), 154.

5. *Environment and Art in Catholic Worship*, par. 29 (Washington, D.C.: National Conference of Catholic Bishops, 1978). Although authorized by Roman Catholic bishops in the United States as a basic document for the building or renovation of churches, this work has had considerable ecumenical influence due to its rich insight into the nature of the liturgy. See also a statement on worship space published by the Episcopal Church, *The Church for Common Prayer* (New York: Episcopal Church Building Fund, 1994).

6. John A. T. Robinson, "Preface," in *Making the Building Serve the Liturgy*, ed. Gilbert Cope (London: A. R. MowGray & Company, 1962), 5.

∾ **Chapter 3: Whose Culture?**

1. See Louis Bouyer, *Rite and Man: The Sense of the Sacral and Christian Liturgy* (London: Burns and Oates, 1963), especially chp. 5, "Phenomenology of Rites: Sacraments and Sacramentals and Their Natural Analogues," pp. 63-77.

2. This question is fully presented in a masterful study by Nathan Mitchell: *Cult and Controversy: The Worship of the Eucharist Outside Mass* (New York: Pueblo Publishing Company, 1982). See especially chp. 3, "Controversy and Estrangement," pp. 66-128.

3. This development corresponded at more or less the same time (ninth century) with the removal of the chalice from the communion of the laity. See Mitchell, *Cult and Controversy*, 96, 117.

4. The most recent publication in this ongoing development is *Enriching Our Worship* (New York: Church Publishing, 1998).

5. See Daniel B. Stevick, *Language in Worship: Reflections in a Crisis* (New York: Seabury Press, 1970). See also the more recent work of Gail Ramshaw, *God Beyond Gender* (Minneapolis: Fortress Press, 1995), and Brian Wren, *What Language Shall I Borrow?* (New York: Crossroad, 1990).

6. See the 1928 *Book of Common Prayer* marriage rite (page 301). Although when used today the phrase is generally not understood in this sense, the words "Who giveth this Woman to be maried to this Man?" are in fact a ritual vestige of a time when the bride was *transferred* from the authority of her father to that of her new husband, not unlike a piece of property.

7. In *Liturgical Piety* (Notre Dame: Notre Dame University Press, 1955), Louis Bouyer gives a thorough historical analysis of this performance model of liturgical celebration which he characterizes as "the

Baroque mentality." See especially chapter 1, "False Conceptions of the Liturgy—Products of the Baroque Period," pp.1-9.

8. Said by Ippolit to Prince Myshkin in *The Idiot* (1868), part III, chp. 5; see also "Nobel Lecture," in *Aleksandr Solzhenitsyn: Critical Essays and Documentary Materials*, ed. J. B. Dunlop, *et al* (Englewood Cliffs, N.J.: Prentice-Hall, 1976), 559.

9. In Anglicanism, this idealization of the Gothic had an extraordinary influence both in England and abroad. See James F. White, *The Cambridge Movement* (Cambridge: Cambridge University Press, 1962) and also the scathing evaluation of the impact of this movement in Kenneth Clark, *The Gothic Revival* (New York: Holt, Rinehart & Winston, 1928).

10. John Paul II, *Ut Unum Sint*, Encyclical Letter on Commitment to Ecumenism (25 May 1995), especially par. 96.

11. See Paul Gibson, "What is the Future Role of Liturgy in Anglican Unity?" in *Liturgical Inculturation in the Anglican Communion*, ed. David R. Holeton, GROW Liturgical Study 15 (Nottingham: Grove Books, 1990), 17-22. See also Phillip Tovey, *Inculturation: The Eucharist in Africa*, GROW Liturgical Study 7 (Nottingham: Grove Books, 1988).

ᴗ Chapter 4: Whose Music?

1. Don Saliers, "The Integrity of Sung Prayer," in *Worship*, 55:4 (July 1981): 290-303. Twenty years after its publication, the article continues to offer essential insight to the nexus between music and the liturgy.

2. Church musicians and other liturgical planners now have available to them a wide variety of resources (especially from Church Publishing) that facilitate the selection of hymns related to the

appointed readings for a particular liturgy. Their use enables a congregation to avoid the pitfall of drawing from too limited and monotonous a selection of hymns from among the rich resources offered by *The Hymnal 1982*.

3. These criteria were spelled out in a document published by the Roman Catholic Bishops' Committee on the Liturgy in 1972, entitled "Music in Catholic Worship." A useful discussion of the criteria as they relate to the place of music in liturgical celebration is presented in paragraphs 23-41.

4. The text of the eucharistic prayer found in *Apostolic Tradition*, for example, does not include a *Sanctus*. See Cuming, *Hippolytus*, par. 4, pp. 10-11. See also Brian D. Spinks, *The Sanctus in the Eucharistic Prayer* (Cambridge: Cambridge University Press, 1991), especially pp. 57-121.

5. I have looked at the question of the inclusion of the Nicene Creed within the eucharistic rite in "Proclamation of Faith in the Eucharist," in *Time and Community*, ed. J. Neil Alexander (Washington, D.C.: The Pastoral Press, 1990), 279-290.

6. Among numerous examples one might note, in England the famous series of sermons delivered by Thomas Bisse, *The Beauty of Holiness in the Common-Prayer* (London: William and John Innys, 1716), and in America, the sermon by the most important churchman in the colonies prior to the Revolution, Samuel Johnson of Connecticut, "The Beauty of Holiness in the Worship of the Church of England" (1749), in *Samuel Johnson, President of King's College: His Career and Writings* (New York: Columbia University Press, 1929), vol. 3, pp. 515-537.

7. The body of apologetical writings on the Anglican liturgy is vast, beginning its long development during the first century of the separation of the English

church from the Church of Rome as various authors sought to defend the theological and liturgical life of the church from the attacks from Geneva on one side and from Rome on the other. Examples of this literature include: Robert Nelson, *A Companion for the Festivals and Fasts of the Church of England*, rev. ed. (London: Thomas Tegg, 1837), and Charles Wheatly, *A Rational Illustration of the Book of Common Prayer*, rev. ed. (Cambridge: The University Press, 1858). A representative sampling of this literature is available in *Prayer Book Spirituality*, ed. J. R. Wright (New York: Church Hymnal Corporation, 1989).

8. I have discussed this issue of the prayer book and Anglican unity more fully in my essay "A Perspective on the Relation of the Prayer Book to Anglican Unity," in *With Ever Joyful Hearts*, ed. J. Neil Alexander (New York: Church Publishing, 1999), 321-332.

9. Examples are numerous, but we might note in particular the dramatic reduction in the amount of water used in baptism from a quantity adequate for an immersion to a small amount adequate only for a sprinkling.

10. See the visionary essay by Thomas Merton, "The General Dance," in *New Seeds of Contemplation* (New York: New Directions, 1962), 290-297.

∼ Chapter 5: Whose Sacraments?

1. Gregory Dix, *The Shape of the Liturgy* (Westminster: Dacre Press, 1945), 744.

2. Louis Bouyer, *Rite and Man: The Sense of the Sacral and Christian Liturgy* (London: Burns and Oates, 1963), 63-77.

3. See the valuable contribution on this question by Michael Amaladoss, S. J., *Do Sacraments Change? Variable and Invariable Elements in Sacramental Rites* (Bangalore: Theological Publications in India, 1979).

4. Consider the phrase in the version of the eucharistic prayer of St. Basil the Great in *The Book of Common Prayer* as Eucharistic Prayer D: "Remember, Lord, your one, holy, catholic and apostolic Church, redeemed by the blood of your Christ. *Reveal its unity*, guard its faith, and preserve it in peace" (BCP 375, italics added).

5. See John A. Gurrieri, "Sacraments Shaping Faith: The Problem of Sacramental Validity Today," in *Fountain of Life*, ed. Gerard Austin (Washington, D.C.: Pastoral Press, 1991), 165-181. Gurrieri offers a useful overview of both historical and theological aspects of the present situation of the church with regard to issues of sacramental validity.

6. Theodor Klauser, *A Short History of the Western Liturgy* (Oxford: Oxford University Press, 1969), 45-84.

7. James F. White, *Documents of Christian Worship* (Louisville: Abingdon, 1992), 147.

8. John Knox, *The Church and the Reality of Christ* (London: Collins, 1963), 10.

9. From the conclusion to Cranmer's Prayer for the Whole State of Christ's Church. See *The Book of Common Prayer*, page 328, and my book *Gathered to Pray* (Cambridge, Mass.: Cowley Publications, 1986).

10. See G. J. Cuming, "Four Very Early Anaphoras," in *Worship* 58:2 (1984): 168-172.

Resources

The twentieth-century Liturgical Movement and the vigorous activity among the various Christian traditions in the reform and renewal of their liturgical rites has led to the publication of a vast literature in the field of liturgical studies. That literature covers the theological and historical issues of this reform, as well as their pastoral implementation in the practice of liturgy in our diverse communities. My intention in this list of additional resources is simply to indicate some recent titles that I think would be valuable for readers who wish to continue further in reading and reflection on the issues raised in this book.

∼ Theology of Worship

Bradshaw, Paul F. *The Search for the Origins of Christian Worship.* New York: Oxford University Press, 1992. (Church of England)

Corbon, Jean. *The Wellspring of Worship.* New York: Paulist Press, 1988. (Roman Catholic)

Lathrop, Gordon. *Holy Things: A Liturgical Theology.* Minneapolis: Fortress Press, 1993. (Lutheran)

Osborne, Kenan B. *Christian Sacraments in a Post-Modern World.* New York: Paulist Press, 1999. (Roman Catholic)

Saliers, Don E. *Worship as Theology.* Nashville: Abingdon Press, 1994. (Methodist)

Weil, Louis. "Prayer, Liturgical." In *The New Dictionary of Sacramental Worship*, ed. Peter Fink, SJ, 949-959. Collegeville, Minn.: Liturgical Press, 1990. (Episcopal)

〜 The Book of Common Prayer

Lee, Jeffrey. *Opening the Prayer Book.* Cambridge, Mass.: Cowley Publications, 1999. (Episcopal)

Moriarty, Michael. *The Liturgical Revolution.* New York: Church Hymnal Corporation, 1996. (Episcopal)

Weil, Louis, and Charles P. Price. *Liturgy for Living.* Revised edition. Harrisburg: Morehouse, 2000. (Episcopal)

Weil, Louis, ed. "Unbound! Anglican Worship Beyond the Prayer Book." *Anglican Theological Review* 82:1 (Winter 2000). (Ecumenical)

〜 Christian Initiation

Holeton, D. R., ed. *Growing in Newness of Life: Christian Initiation in Anglicanism Today.* Toronto: The Anglican Book Centre, 1993. (Anglican Church of Canada)

Meyers, Ruth A. *Continuing the Reformation: Re-Visioning Baptism in the Episcopal Church.* New York: Church Publishing, 1997. (Episcopal)

Stevick, Daniel. *Baptismal Moments; Baptismal Meanings.* New York: Church Hymnal Corporation, 1987. (Episcopal)

〜 The Holy Eucharist

Crockett, William R. *Eucharist: Symbol of Transformation.* (New York: Pueblo Publishing Company, 1989. (Anglican Church of Canada)

Holeton, D.R., ed. *Our Thanks and Praise: The Eucharist in Anglicanism Today.* Toronto: The Anglican Book Centre, 1998. (Anglican Church of Canada)

Leonard, J. K. and Nathan D. Mitchell. *The Postures of the Assembly During the Eucharistic Prayer.* Chicago: Liturgy Training Publications, 1994. (Roman Catholic)

Stevenson, K. *Eucharist and Offering.* New York: Pueblo Publishing Company, 1986. (Church of England)

∼ The People of God

Countryman, L. William. *Living on the Border of the Holy.* Harrisburg: Morehouse Publishing, 1999. (Episcopal)

Fairless, Caroline. *Children at Worship: Congregations in Bloom.* New York: Church Publishing, 2000. (Episcopal)

Lathrop, Gordon. *Holy People: A Liturgical Ecclesiology.* Minneapolis: Fortress Press, 1999. (Lutheran)

Meyers, Ruth A., ed. *Children at the Table.* New York: Church Publishing, 1995. (Episcopal)

Smith, Elizabeth J. *Bearing Fruit in Due Season. Feminist Hermeneutics and the Bible in Worship.* Collegeville, Minn.: Liturgical Press, 1999. (Anglican Church of Australia)

Questions for Group Discussion

∿ **Chapter 1: Which Theology?**

1. What are some of the reasons you attend church services? Do you think of your attendance as optional? a matter of individual choice? a religious or social obligation?

2. Weil notes that "our public worship reveals how we understand ourselves as the church." Do you agree? Think of a particular liturgy in your congregation, such as the way you celebrate the eucharist or a baptism. What does this liturgy reveal about your common life as a parish?

3. Reflecting on the worship, outreach, and pastoral life in your own congregation, how would you answer the question posed in this chapter, "Which theology—baptismal or clerical?"

∿ **Chapter 2: Who Celebrates?**

1. When you look at your Sunday bulletin, what does it tell you about the ministries and ministers in your congregation? How would you describe your own role

in worship? How would you answer the question, "Who celebrates?"

2. In this chapter Weil discusses the importance of worship for the identity of the church as the body of Christ. He notes: "Our gathering is not primarily a matter of function but rather of identity: the whole body of the baptized constitutes itself in diverse communities around the world." In what specific ways has worship in community shaped your identity as a Christian? as a member of a congregation?

3. In what ways do you "encounter the sacred" in your church? How do you think your church building affects your corporate worship? your congregational identity and ministries?

～ Chapter 3: Whose Culture?

1. How has your cultural background, and the culture in which you now live, affected your Christian faith? How have they shaped your experience of beauty in worship?

2. How does your congregation respond to the question, "Whose culture?" What cultures are represented among the members of your congregation? How are these cultures given expression in the liturgy, and how are such decisions made?

3. Weil asserts that "the characteristics of our Anglican heritage that we most cherish will live into the future of the church not as fossils of the past but through their *incarnation* in the widely diverse cultures of our world." Which characteristics of Anglicans do you cherish the most? How might they

need to adapt and change within a multicultural church?

～ Chapter 4: Whose Music?

1. Do you agree with Don Saliers that "liturgy is inherently musical"? What role has music played in your life of prayer? What kinds of music are used in your church's worship? Which kinds do you think are successful expressions of the community's prayer? Which are not? Why?

2. Apply the musical, liturgical, and pastoral criteria Weil sets out in this chapter to the musical dimension of worship in your congregation. How would you describe the quality of the music you hear and sing? Does the music in the liturgy fit its intended function? Is it appropriate for your particular congregation? Why or why not?

3. How is prayer "embodied" in your congregation? In what ways are movements limited or circumscribed by your traditions or your church building? How does your congregation respond to people who move "too much" (children) and to people whose movements are impaired (the handicapped and elderly)? Can you envision ways that different expressions of move-ment—dance, processions, gestures—could be incor-porated into the liturgy in your congregation?

～ Chapter 5: Whose Sacraments?

1. Weil states that "when we turn to consider the sacraments of Christian baptism and eucharist, we see that they are based upon universal experiences shared by all human beings." Have you experienced times in which ordinary human moments—meals, washing, touching—have seemed to be sacred moments as well?

Did you recognize them as sacramental at the time? What were the criteria you used?

2. What do you think it means for the sacraments to be "instituted by Christ"?

3. How has your reading and discussion of this book changed your understanding of liturgy? What specific changes would you like to see in the worship life of your congregation?

Cowley Publications is a ministry of the Society of St. John the Evangelist, a religious community for men in the Episcopal Church. Emerging from the Society's tradition of prayer, theological reflection, and diversity of mission, the press is centered in the rich heritage of the Anglican Communion.

Cowley Publications seeks to provide books, CDs, audio cassettes, and other resources for the ongoing theological exploration and spiritual development of the Episcopal Church and others in the body of Christ. To this end, it is dedicated to developing a new generation of theological writers, encouraging them to produce timely, creative, and stimulating publications of excellence, and making these publications available widely, reaching both clergy and lay persons.